G000293582

LORD HARRIS'S TEAM IN AUSTRALIA 1878-79

THE DIARY OF VERNON ROYLE

1. Portrait of Vernon Royle.
Reproduced from *Cricket* Magazine, April 16, 1885

THE MCC CRICKET LIBRARY

LORD HARRIS'S TEAM IN AUSTRALIA 1878 – 79

The Diary of Vernon Royle

With
Match Reports and Scores
(Reprinted from *Wisden's Cricketers' Almanack* for 1880)

Introduction
by
GERALD HOWAT

MCC in conjunction with J.W. McKenzie
2001

The extract from *John Wisden's Cricketers' Almanack for 1880* reprinted by kind permission of
John Wisden and Company Limited.

ISBN 0 947821 10 4

Printed by
E & E Plumridge Ltd
Linton Cambridge CB1 6HS

CONTENTS

LIST OF ILLUSTRATIONS

FOREWORD

The Diary of Vernon Royle's visit to Australia in 1878-79 and his completion of a round-the-world journey is in the possession of the Royle family. A copy has been presented to the Marylebone Cricket Club Library.

MCC acknowledges with thanks the permission of the family to reproduce the text of the diary.

The account of the cricket tour itself, led by Lord Harris, is reprinted from the 1880 edition of *Wisden's Cricketers' Almanack* by kind permission of John Wisden and Company Limited.

This book forms a contribution to the publishing programme of the MCC Arts and Library sub-committee. I commend it to cricket enthusiasts and collectors alike.

Ted Dexter
President, MCC

Introduction

By Gerald Howat

The tourists who visited Australia in 1878-79 under the captaincy of Lord Harris were the fifth such cricket party to go there from England in the 1860s and 1870s. It had been George Parr's team to North America in 1859 which had pioneered the concept of overseas tours and it may be useful to notice the factors which encouraged those to Australia over this period.

The development of the steam ship – the *Great Britain* had taken the team to Australia in 1861 – and, later, the opening of the Suez Canal, eventually reduced the passage to two months. By the 1860s the Australian cities of Melbourne and Sydney were enjoying economic prosperity with entrepreneurial business men seeing profits in promoting cricket teams from "the old country". The game itself was developing fast encouraged by colonial governors such as Sir William Denison of New South Wales who allocated part of Sydney's Domain to be a cricket ground. This was linked to the concept of an Empire bounded by mutual ties, among which were those of cricket. It is a truism which has recognisable overtones in a twenty-first century Commonwealth.

Crowds of many thousands flocked to see the English players – 30,000 at Sydney in 1874 – and such was the popularity of the game that standards improved, English professionals were employed, and the two countries were able to compete on equal terms at Melbourne in 1877 in what has been adjudged, retrospectively, as the first-ever Test match. All this is to see things from an Australian perspective.

In mid-nineteenth century England there were professional cricketers, some with similar entrepreneurial ambitions to the Australian business men, who saw there was a regular and substantial income to be gained by spending the English winters in Australia – as well as in New Zealand and North America. Knowing their financial worth, players would drive hard bargains before agreeing to tour. There were also amateurs, usually the products of the major public schools and of Oxford and Cambridge where cricket had reached comparatively high standards by 1860. Such men might have the leisure and personal resources to travel although for some, such as

Vernon Royle, our diarist, a tour would be the trip of a life-time.

Distinct from both these groups was the unique figure of W.G. Grace. A syndicate, after two years of haggling, agreed to his demands of £1,500 and the expenses of himself and his wife to take a side out to Australia in 1873. The professionals whom he recruited (with some difficulty) got £170 each. This is not the place to discuss the status of Grace whom *Lillywhite's Companion* called a "gentleman professional" and whose position *Wisden*, in 1878, called "an anomaly".

The four visiting teams to Australia which preceded that of Harris were made up largely of professionals and, allowing some qualification for Grace, captained by one. All the tours had been beneficial to the sponsors and all had left the paid players with upwards of £150 each. On Grace's tour they augmented their income by selling cricket equipment and by betting. James Lillywhite's tour of 1876-77 was the first in which the speculation of making a profit was an English enterprise rather than an Australian one, with Lillywhite displaying a business zeal which others, such as Alfred Shaw and Arthur Shrewsbury, would emulate in the 1880s. Financial success depended on the response of the Australian cricketing public, something which may be summed up in the report sent to London by the Australian correspondent of *The Times* in January 1864 and printed in the edition of March 14.

> Our southern sun is at its fiercest and society watches with breathless interest the changing fortunes of the "All England Eleven". The cricket fever has been raging for the last month. Are we never to read the last of Parr's cricketing perfections? Silver coinage must be plentiful when £2,500 were taken in half-crowns for entrance to the Melbourne ground on New Year's Day.

It was into such a climate of sunshine and enthusiasm that the English cricketers, led by Lord Harris,[1] arrived in Australia in December 1878. They had left a very different homeland in October, where a long winter of ice, snow and wind was about to begin.

1. Harris wrote an account of the tour in *Lillywhite's Cricket Annual* for 1880.

Matches on ice would be recorded in *Wisden* which also declared, more starkly, that the land had been "sorely stricken with distress, disease and death". Of all this, they could scarcely have been aware until the mails arrived.

Harris's tourists differed from the preceding four teams in that the party was almost entirely composed of amateurs. The original invitation from the Melbourne Cricket Club had been sent to the Middlesex amateur, I.D. Walker. Unable, for family reasons, to respond (although later joining the team in Australia but not playing), he had asked Harris to assume responsibility for raising, captaining and managing the side – which was strengthened by two professionals.

We should say something about these players, their credentials and their later careers. The fourth Baron Harris (1851-1932), far from being the greatest cricketer of his generation, was nevertheless, the most influential one over some sixty years. He captained England in the first home Test, in 1880, and played for Kent for over forty years, making his last appearance at the age of 60. His final match, took place at his old school, Eton, when he was 79. Less important, in the broader scheme of things, were the 9,990 runs he made (26.85) and the 190 catches he took in first-class cricket. On the great cricketing issues of his day, such as throwing, the authority of the laws and the status of professionals, he pronounced uncompromisingly. He was at once an idealist and an autocrat who ruled the corridors of Kent and MCC as a man for his times. After being president of MCC in 1895, he served as treasurer from 1896 till 1932. Cricket apart, he held political office and was Governor of Bombay (1890-95). In the last year of his life, he declared that to play cricket "kindly, humbly, generously, self-sacrificingly (was) a moral lesson in itself". They were words turned bitter-sweet by the bodyline bowling controversy which broke out a few months after his death. Not long before his own death in 2000 E.W. Swanton was helping in the re-arrangement of portraits in the Long Room at Lord's. He paused at that of Harris and recalled looking with some awe at the great man in that same place some seventy years earlier. So do cricket memories span the ages.

Two others who would make their mark as players and administrators were A.N. Hornby (1847-1925) and A.J. Webbe (1855-1941). Both men had played in the famous game at Lord's in the preceding summer in which the Australians had beaten MCC in a single day, after Spofforth had had a match analysis of eleven for 20. Hornby would later lead England twice (with Grace under him). He also appeared for his country nine times at rugby football. He was an attacking batsman who captained Lancashire by example, making over 16,000 runs in his career. Between 1870 and 1881, when no other Lancastrian made a century, he contributed seven. Later he served for many years as county president. He has been immortalised in the haunting lines of the poet Francis Thompson:

> As the run-stealers flicker to and fro, to and fro,
> O my Hornby and my Barlow long ago.

Webbe, like others of his generation and background, had the leisure and the independence to devote himself entirely to cricket's welfare. He served both MCC and Middlesex for nearly seventy years, being a trustee of the former and president of the latter. Although his appearance at Melbourne in 1879 for Harris' team proved to be his only Test match, he scored over 14,000 runs in first-class cricket – mostly for Middlesex. To have taken six catches in an innings for the Gentlemen in 1877 and have made 243 against Yorkshire in 1887 were no mean achievements. Although war-time *Wisdens* were thin productions, that of 1942 (a collector's item) found the space to devote three pages to his memory, a man "with a wonderfully, kind nature".

Three who would make more modest contributions to the game were A.P. Lucas (1857-1923), Frank Penn (1851-1925) and F.A. MacKinnon (1848-1947). Lucas, the youngest of the tourists, had just come down from Cambridge where he had been regarded as the leading batsman of the 1878 University side which had won all its matches. As a schoolboy at Uppingham, under the coaching of H.H. Stephenson – who had taken the first side to Australia in 1861 – he had been hailed as a "new star" and been selected for the Gentlemen of the South a few days after leaving school. With Grace, at the Oval in 1880, he shared in the first century partnership in Test cricket. Four years later, however, on the same ground when England lost to the Australians by seven runs, his relentless orthodox defence possibly denied victory when a boundary or two would have broken in the stranglehold of Spofforth's bowling. In a spasmodic career spanning 33 years, mostly with Essex, work commitments never allowed him to fulful the early expectations. Penn was called in his *Wisden* obituary "the most famous Kent batsman of a generation back". His one Test appearance, at the Oval in 1880, gave him a career average of 50.00 at that level, but within a year he was required to give up the game on medical advice. Subsequently, he was president of Kent.

The 35th MacKinnon of MacKinnon, as he became in 1903, was the oldest survivor of the party. No other first-class cricketer had lived as long as he when he died shortly before his 99th birthday. He retained a life-long interest in the game and E.W. Swanton, meeting him in 1946, recorded his warm memories of his only Test – Melbourne in 1879 – and noticed him still wearing the watch-chain with crossed bats which Harris had given to his players. He was three months senior to Grace. It is a whimsical thought that if the Great Cricketer himself had lived to a similar age, he might have commented on such Test debutants as Alec Bedser and Godfrey Evans. After Cambridge MacKinnon played for Kent for ten years, scoring centuries against Yorkshire and Hampshire.

Our next pair, Charles Absolom (1846-89) and S.S. Schultz (1857-1937), did not contribute a great deal to the game after their return from Australia but each has his own interest. Absolom, of all the tourists, was the most colourful, not least because he wore a red shirt on his debut at Lord's in 1866. In appearance, he looked extraordinarily like Grace who said of him "he was worthy of a place in any eleven for the excellent and stimulating example he showed". *Scores and Biographies* called him "a hard, lively and eccentric hitter". In what proved to be his only Test, he scored a half-century at Melbourne yet he had not enjoyed the tour. To a friend he wrote: "I have a schoolboy's list of days until we return, and religiously strike off one every morning – it's my one ray of sunshine". Absolom was a lovesick swain whose suit, when he returned to England, was unrequited. He played one last game for Kent and took himself off to America to live among Indian tribes for ten years before signing on as purser on the SS "Muriel" plying between New York and Trinidad. His end was as bizarre as his life: he was killed by a crane loading sugar at Port of Spain.

Schultz, like Absolom, a Cambridge Blue, made very occasional appearances for Lancashire up to 1882. He had an unusual claim to fame in having been dismissed first ball twice in the first innings of the same match. He was playing for the Gentlemen versus Oxford University at Christ Church in 1881 when the match was abandoned, shortly after his dismissal, because of the "hard and lumpy state of the ground". The players then took cabs to the Parks and started again upon which Schultz (normally a lower-order batsman) was again out. Some years before the outbreak of war in 1914 – although a North countryman by birth – he deemed it prudent to change his surname to Storey.

The remaining amateurs – of what was intended to be a side of "Gentlemen" – were Leland Hone (1853-96) and Henry Maul (1850-1940). Hone was a last-minute selection as wicket-keeper though he had had little experience in the role. He had made first-class appearances against both Universities in the preceding summer without keeping wicket. He had played for Ireland for four years and was of a well-known Irish cricketing family but he himself would play no more at first-class level after the tour. Maul, alone of the players with no first-class cricket to his name, was a free-hitting batsman for Warwickshire in the county's second-class days. Most notably, he would make 267 against Staffordshire in 1888.

The two Yorkshire professionals, secured to strengthen a very weak attack, were George Ulyett (1851-98) and Tom Emmett (1841-1904). Both had already visited Australia with Lillywhite's team in 1876-77 and both had played in what became the first Test match. Ulyett, who began his working life in the pits in Yorkshire, was born and died at Pitsmoor, near Sheffield. With three more visits to Australia, together with ones to New Zealand, South Africa and North America, he would be the most travelled cricketer of his generation. *Cricket* estimated he spent 157,000 miles at sea. Recruited by Harris primarily as a bowler, Ulyett was also the leading Yorkshire batsman of his day. He played in 25 of England's first 33 Test matches, and, in first-class cricket, scored over 20,000 runs and took over 650 wickets. His seven for 36 in 39 overs brought England a notable victory at Lord's in 1884, a ground where he once hit a six over the (old) pavilion. "Happy Jack" earned a reasonable living from cricket. His overseas' tours brought him, on average, £200 each and in his will he left over £1,000.

Emmett went on to make seven appearances for England although none of them at home. He had begun as a left-arm fast bowler, later turning to spin. He bowled 60,333 balls for his 1,571 wickets in first-class cricket with the redoubtable average of 13.56. Although a professional, he had captained Yorkshire in the pre-Lord Hawke days. Indeed, the concept of the amateur captain belongs more to the first sixty years of the twentieth century than to any other time. Emmett, a man of character and personality, once addressed his fielders, "there's an epidemic but it isn't catching". After retirement he became coach at Rugby School playing a major part in the development of the 15-year old "Plum" Warner as a 1st XI batsman.

We have left to the last Vernon Royle (1854-1929) whose diary of the tour gave rise to this book. He was the son of a Manchester doctor and had been an outstanding athlete at Rossall School, making his debut for Lancashire at the age of nineteen. Going up to Brasenose College, Oxford, he won his Blue in 1875 and 1876 and established himself as an outstanding cover-point. *Cricket*, in 1896, would call him "without doubt the most famous of them all". Part of his skill lay in being ambidextrous in his throw. His fellow-tourist, Emmett, knew him of old. In a Roses match, he sent back his Yorkshire partner with the cry, "Woa, there's a policeman". Royle already had a double-century in minor cricket to his credit and in the year he went to Australia had come second in the Lancashire batting averages. He would make 31 for the Gentlemen versus the Players in 1882.

His diary of the trip round the world – for so it proved with two unofficial matches in New Zealand and the United States - is a narrative of what he saw, whom he met and how the team played. It presents the uncomplicated adventures of a young man who did not take himself too seriously. He enjoyed the tour as much for the friends he made as for the cricket he played and it is a social comment on the times in which he lived.

On returning home he became a master – later headmaster – at Elstree preparatory school in Hertfordshire and took Holy Orders in 1881, serving his title at Aldenham parish church. Both Elstree and Stanmore school (which he founded in 1901) became nurseries of Harrow, University and county cricketers. In 1885, for example, eight of the Harrow XI had been at Elstree while Stanmore sent more cricketers to Harrow, in his time, than did any other preparatory school.

Royle married Eleanor Sanderson in 1885. Their four sons all went to Harrow while four grandsons were to be seen at the Eton and

Harrow match at Lord's in 2000. Royle was elected president of Lancashire in 1929 and died during his year of office, on May 20, aged 75. To the end of his life he was an active headmaster, regarded, as his obituarist wrote, "with real affection (who) treated all who came into contact with him as his friends and equals".

This was the man who opened his diary on October 17, 1878, to record that "the English team left from Southampton for 'Australia' to play several cricket matches there".

The Diary of Vernon Royle
17th October 1878 – 11 May 1879

Diary from 17th October 1878, the day the English team left England from Southampton for Australia to play several cricket matches there per P & O SS "Australia". Capt. Cates.

Oct. 17th Thursday

Left Southampton about 3.15 by the P & O Steamship "Australia". Cambell (*sic*) Hulton came down to see us off. Had a beautiful day for starting and continued fine.

Oct. 18th Friday

Got up in the morning, the ship rolling very much, felt very uncomfortable and had to part with what little I had "on board". Went to my berth and stayed there all day, not feeling at all well. In the night a rat ate the side out of my boot, rather a good beginning. It ran over Maul while he was in bed, Maul being in the same cabin with me. Our cabin was 148-149, 150 & 151. Schultz and Lucas in a two berthed cabin next and Absolom and MacKinnon[2] next to them in a 4 berthed cabin.

Oct. 19th Saturday.

Continued very unwell, ship rolling as much as ever, ate very little all day and drank still less.

Oct. 20th Sunday.

Rather worse than ever. No breakfast, lunch or dinner, only a hard biscuit and a bun. Had service in Saloon, Capt. Cates officiating. In the evening a heavy rain storm, accompanied by thunder and lightning. Slept very badly, the ship rolling very much and Maul snoring fearfully.

Oct. 21st Monday.

Weather much calmer, but still not able to go down to meals, endeavoured to take lunch but had to hook it before I had finished. Wrote a letter home to my mother, also scribbled a few lines to Teddy Rowley. Rougher again at night.

Oct. 22nd Tuesday.

Arrived at Gibraltar about 6.45 a.m. Went ashore at once and had breakfast at the "Royal". Met Willie Walker there, who had just landed,

2. *Wisden* spells MacKinnon with a small 'k'

being on his way to Genoa, also young Campbell of the Rifle Brigade. Left Gibraltar again about 10.30 and weighed anchor for Malta at 11.15. The weather was beautiful, scarcely a ripple on the sea. Gibraltar and the Bay looked very pretty as we left it.

Oct. 23rd Wednesday.
Had a very good night and partook of breakfast for the first time on board. The weather still continuing nice and the sea smooth. Awning hung all round the vessel. In the evening an endeavour was made to get up a dance which resulted in a failure. No one being able or at any rate willing to play the piano, which had been hauled on deck. Passed Algiers about 8 o'clock in the evening.

Oct. 24th Thursday.
Still just in sight of land. Beautiful day, the sun being very hot. Wrote a letter to my father, which is to be posted at Malta. In the evening we had some singing etc. after the ladies had retired, in which a 2nd class passenger joined, he was very good, his best song being one called "Sour Crowt" or some such name. Saw flying fish for the first time.

Oct. 25th Friday.
Sea beautifully calm, passed the Island of Pantelleria about 9 a.m. Scarcely a ripple on the sea. Can just make out the outline of the coast of Sicily, at least so I am told. Passed Gozo and arrived at Valetta about 8.30 p.m. It was very curious to see the lights of the small boats following and going alongside of us as we steamed slowly up the harbour. As soon as we were hove to, the medical officer came alongside and boarded us, before which nobody was allowed to leave the ship. Directly he had departed, or at any rate when we were at liberty to go, the boats came round in swarms, the boatmen making a most infernal din, jabbering like so many monkeys. At length we got away and were rowed ashore, and landed at the "Marsa Mucet", or some such name. There were swarms of Maltese waiting for us, and as soon as we landed they surrounded us and wanted to act as guides. We engaged one and then set off. Before getting into the town we had to ascend a large number of steps. It was late by this time viz nearly 9.15, however all the shops were open. We first paid a visit to some of them, but I made no purchases and as the opera house happened to be open

and the opera of "Norma" going on, we decided to go and have a look at it. We had to pay 2 shillings each and got a very good seat. It is a splendid building; the body of it being filled with arm chairs. There is no dress circle, gallery etc., but every available space from floor to ceiling is given up to small boxes. Met Cornish of the 33rd and Rawlinson. After the opera was over, Maul and I went with them to the club house, where we had supper etc. Arrived back on board about 1 o'clock. A most infernal din was going on, as they were coaling when we arrived.

Oct. 26th Saturday.
Went onshore again about 6.30 a.m. with MacKinnon and Lucas, engaged the same guide, who took us to St. John's Church, a magnificent building, the floor being of marble in oblong blocks, and each block, with an inscription on the top, forming the gravestone of an ancient Knight of Malta. At the end, over the Altar, are two beautiful figures, very large, carved out of the solid marble. The ceiling is elaborately painted, had not much time to lose, so went to the Palace. This also is a beautiful pile of buildings. Entered by a flight of marble steps. The tapestry in the council chamber is very good, being 200 years old. The armoury is also well worth seeing. As we had to be on board before 9 o'clock, it was time to prepare for leaving, so we bought some fruit and took our departure. The streets of Malta are very narrow and run parallel to one another being intersected by others also parallel, thus the town is made up of square blocks of buildings. Had a beautiful view over the Grand Harbour, the "Serapis" and "Tamar" lying at anchor. The former left about 1/2 hour before us for Suez, but we overtook her very soon. The Maltese are a regular swindling lot, trying to palm off dollars etc. for shillings, consequently one has to be on the look out. They *always* ask double for anything they want to sell and very often will take less than half of the price they originally asked.

Oct. 27th Sunday.
Weather still fine. Captain read the service on deck.

Oct. 28th Monday.
In the morning saw some curious objects out to sea, supposed to be the fins of sharks, but nobody was certain. Played cricket in the afternoon,

but it was fearfully hot. Concert given in the evening in aid of the Merchant Seamen's Orphan Asylum. Nearly £26 was collected, one gentleman gave 10 guineas.

Oct. 29th Tuesday.
Weather still fine and sea smooth. The coast of Egypt just visible (9.45 a.m.).Arrived at Port Said about 5.30 p.m. Some of our fellows went ashore in the evening, did not go myself. Our passage across the Mediterranean accomplished without a single rough day. The weather was beautiful all the way from Gibraltar. Took in coal.

Oct. 30th Wednesday.
Left Port Said at 6.15 a.m. Got up and saw the sun rise. Entered the Canal directly afterwards. Lake Menzaleh is on the right at the entrance and the desert on the left. Soon after starting, a mirage was visible on the desert. The effect is very curious, a short distance from the side of the canal, there appears to be water and a little further, and as it were standing out of the water, some islands. The illusion continues for some way. We passed myriads of pelicans on the right and further on about 20 miles from Port Said, heaps of flamingoes. The latter are very pretty birds, having black wings, red bodies behind and white necks. Just passed (11 o'clock a.m.) El-Kantara a small village on the banks. It is here where passengers change for Jerusalem. There were about 50 camels or more, huddled together on the shore. Bye the bye, there is scarcely any shore visible when you get to Port Said. The land is so flat and appears only a few inches above the sea level.

At 3.45 p.m. we passed a troupe of Arabs, accompanied by women, children and camels, the latter were very much frightened on hearing the sound of the whistle and jumped about like anything, one of the Arabs being thrown. At 4 o'clock we reached Ismailia just before the bitter lakes. It was here where the Viceroy entertained the Prince of Wales etc. on the opening of the Canal. His Palace is close to the shore (right hand) of the Canal and is a large square looking building, very plain. Just run ashore, no prospect of getting off as yet. 4.15 o'clock p.m. 8.30 Still ashore. Lighters alongside taking off the Bombay luggage.

Oct. 31st Thursday.
Remained fast ashore till 11.30 a.m. in Lac Timsah. Got off after great difficulty. Could not reach Suez the same evening so had to anchor in the Canal about 8 miles off.

Nov. 1st Friday.
Arrived at Suez about 8.30 a.m. Went ashore after breakfast, got a boat and sailed round to the town, about 4 miles off by sea. The town is 2 miles inland from where the ships are moored, but the harbour for small boats runs right up to the town, the landing being at the English Hotel, we arrived there about 12.30 and had lunch there, for which they charged us 4 shillings, a fearful swindle, bottle of beer was 1s 6d extra. The town is a very curious place. No regular streets, all being of loose sand. The women walk about with a kind of domino on, consisting of a kind of screw of gold from the forehead to the bridge of the nose and before that a covering of silk. The men are as a rule married about 14 years old, the girls as young as nine and in some cases less. The man has nothing whatever to do with choosing his new wife. It is all done by his parents. When he is in a position to marry his parents go to the parents of a girl they think suited and buy their child as it were from them. After the marriage a woman is not allowed out of the house without a written permission from her husband. We stayed there some little time looking about the place which is about as miserable a hole as I was ever in. The men are a fine looking lot, very powerful and well made as a rule or at least they appeared so. We rode back to the ship on donkeys which was great fun. It is quite the thing at Suez to ride on donkeys. Were not able to leave that evening as the mails did not come on board until 1 o'clock a.m. Webb and Hone joined us from Brindisi. "Serapis" left at 6 p.m.

Nov. 2nd Saturday.
Left Suez about 6.am.
Received a letter from the Mater. Could see the position of Sinai in the afternoon on the left. Had a dance in the evening.

Nov. 3rd Sunday.
Still beautiful weather, but very hot. Had service on deck at 11.a.m.

Nov. 4th Monday.
Weather still fine. Nothing going on.

Nov. 5th Tuesday.
[no entry].

Nov. 6th Wednesday.
Arrived at Aden about 10.30 p.m. Did not go ashore. Looked a very desolate place in the moonlight.

Nov. 7th Thursday.
Weighed anchor about 5.45 a.m. for Galle[3] A most beautiful morning. Saw the sun rise.

Nov. 8th Friday.
Nothing particular. Sea began to get unsettled.

Nov. 9th Saturday.
Began to blow pretty hard. Was ill twice before breakfast. Was very seedy all day. In the evening saw a lunar rainbow. Dorling caught a flying fish.

Nov. 10th Sunday.
Sea calmer but still rough. Felt worse than ever, but was not ill.
The moon shone on the water very curiously in the evening about 8 o'clock.

11th Monday.
Thank goodness the fine weather has returned. Felt myself again.

Nov. 12th Tuesday.
Capt. Parry thought he saw a Nautilus early this morning, did not see it myself. Expect to reach Galle on Friday. Mrs. Hornby[4] not at all well. Saw another lunar rainbow.

Nov. 13th Wednesday.
Very nice day and sea smooth. Played penny nap in the afternoon with

3. In Ceylon.
4. Lord Harris and A.N. Hornby took their wives on the tour.

MacKinnon and Miss Ingram.[5] Rather fun. Was very much amused when told that Mrs. De P – s had reported 3rd Officer (B – t) for flirting with Miss W – n.

Nov. 14th Thursday.
Mails taken up from the hold, tremendous lot of them. Little Tommy, the barber, was locked up in the bath room, for nearly an hour this morning, by the bar-man. He was very angry.

Nov. 15th Friday.
Arrived at Galle about 6.30 a.m. Waited for breakfast on board the "Australia", and then took my luggage across to the "Assam". There is always a heavy swell in the Harbour. After taking my luggage (bye the bye it was before breakfast) and seeing our new berth (no. 77-80) a very good cabin on the starboard side forward, Maul being with me, I returned to the "Australia" for breakfast. We left the "Australia" for good about 11 o'clock, went on board the "Assam" and afterwards to the shore. The boats are very curious, called 'catamarans' only wide enough to hold one abreast. On the starboard side 2 poles are extended and at the ends a cross piece lying on the water, so it is impossible to upset. On landing we got a guide, and went to the Oriental Hotel, afterwards we engaged a carriage and drove it to "Wak-Wallah" a few miles out. The country was most beautiful and the foliage of the trees superb. We passed many groves of cocoa nut trees, and bananas.

When about half way to Wak-Wallah, we stopped at a small hut. 2 of the sons could speak English very well. One of the natives climbed up a cocoa nut tree, a sight well worth seeing. The ankles are fastened a little way apart with a grass band, the native then takes hold of the tree as high as he can reach and seems to clasp the trunk with his feet. He then slips his hands up and pulls his feet after him as it were, standing out from the tree all the time. There are no branches on the tree at all, except just at the top. We had some cocoa nut milk and then went on. We were followed all the way by children, wanting to sell flowers and small bunches of fruit, sugar cane, etc. On arriving at the foot of Wak-Wallah, we got out and walked. There was a fine view from the top, the

5. Miss Ingram appears with them in the team photograph.

country underneath being very wet and damp, as it was the rainy season. The valley was nearly all covered with rice, being very much like young wheat in England. There were heaps of natives trying to sell precious stones etc. It is not safe to buy them, unless one is up to it, as very many are coloured glass. The tortoiseshell is very beautiful. The natives wear turbans and a covering round the loins only, except the women who are covered with a loose sheet. Some of the men wear the latter too, and it is very difficult to tell the sexes. Some of the men are very good looking but the women are hideous.

We arrived back again at 2.30 and went on board. Some merchants came on board later on with large cases of rings, etc. The right hand side and head of the harbour is covered with palm trees and on the left is the English church, just peeping out of the trees, which are of a different kind. The gums and lips of the natives are quite of a bright red colour, owing to their eating the leaf of the bettle nut tree. We weighed anchor about 7 p.m. and gave three cheers for the "Australia" as we left, which they returned. There was a heavy swell on, but I was not ill. A sea came into our cabin, so the ports were shut up.

Nov. 16th Saturday.
Very rough and consequently I was very ill, both before and after breakfast. Many of the cocoa nut trees in Galle were bound round about half way up with a dried cocoa nut leaf about 6 feet or more in length. This is intended to keep thieves away at night, as a dry crackling sound is made if anyone attempts to climb the tree.

Nov. 17th Sunday
Still a very nasty sea on. Crossed the Equator about 9 a.m. No ceremony took place. The Bishop of Christ Church, New Zealand (Harper) read the service at 11 o'clock and gave a short address.

Nov. 18th Monday.
Sea smoother but still a long rolling motion.Felt better but not at all myself. They tell me I look *very* well, which is annoying. Capt. McMeekan saw a shark in the afternoon.

Nov. 19th Tuesday.
Roll still continues but feel better.

Nov. 20th Wednesday.
Wretched.

Nov. 21st Thursday.
Ditto.

Nov. 22nd Friday.
Sea rather calmer, but still a heavy swell on.

Nov. 23rd Saturday.
Feel much better, getting used to the continual motion. Enjoyed my food, which is quite the exception. Two flying fishes came on board.

Nov. 24th Sunday.
Very rough night. Bishop Harper read the service and took his text from the VI Chap of John *viz* "and when these men had seen the miracle which Jesus did" etc.

Nov. 25th Monday.
Sea very much smoother, wind gone down. Bitterly cold in the evening, so cold that many of us put Ulsters on.

Nov. 26th Tuesday.
Calmer still. Now out of the "Trades" so hope to have a fair wind. Married and single had a tug of war in the evening. The latter won easily.

Nov. 27th Wednesday.
Got a fair wind and are now going under sail about 12 knots. Sea getting rougher. In the afternoon a cloud appeared on the horizon which soon spread over the sky, and a strong wind ensued, which lashed the waves into foam. The ports were all shut and the awning taken down. Every prospect of rough weather, but it cleared considerably in the evening. Saw a Molly Hawk a bird very much like an albatross.

Nov. 28th Thursday.
Got up early in the morning about 7 a.m. Land visible on the port bow, our first glimpse of Australia. King George's Sound about 100 miles off, hope to get there about 4 o'clock p.m.

Arrived at the Sound about 4.30 p.m. Went ashore. Very little to be seen. Climbed the hill on the right of the "Town" with Lucas, Schultz and MacKinnon. Wrote to the Pater. Returned on board in time for dinner which was postponed from 6 o'clock till 8. The aborigines were a most infernal looking set. Their faces painted all colours, most of them being discoloured with ocre, etc. Weighed anchor about 9 p.m.
Harris received a telegram from Melbourne (I think) saying that 3 of the Committee of the Melbourne Club would meet us at Adelaide etc.

Nov. 29th Friday.
Saw heaps of albatross, followed the ship all day. In the afternoon we were fortunate enough to see 3 or 4 whales, one being a very large one off the starboard quarter. We saw nearly the whole of its body, except the head, its tail standing up far out of the water when it dived. Played tennis with Miss Ingram.

Nov. 30th Saturday.
Beautiful morning but wind right ahead. Only two more days to Adelaide.

Dec. 1st Sunday.
[no entry].

Dec. 2nd Monday.
Passed the "Siam" about 9 a.m. Sighted land about 11 o'clock. Arrived off Glenelg at 10.30 p.m. Met on board by Loughman, Croaker and Robinson.[6] Landed about 12 in a small team tug. 3 drags waiting for us. Drove to Adelaide, 7 miles off. Left Hornby and Harris with the ladies at the "Crown and Sceptre" and drove on to the "Clarence" where we were to be located, in King William St. Post Office on left Town Hall on right. Arrived at 2.15 a.m. Were cheered by a few of the newspaper hands on our arrival, Were very well treated, supper being prepared for us, which we did full justice to.

Dec. 3rd Tuesday.
Got up very early as we had to be presented to the Mayor (Mr. Scott of

6. All of the Melbourne C.C. Augustus Robinson was responsible in 1892 for the inauguration of the Sheffield Shield to be competed for by the Australian colonies.

Mount Lofty) at 10.30. He received us very kindly and Harris responded. Wound up the interview with drinking each other's health. Were driven round the town afterwards by Hart and Stirling. Lunched at the club and went to the ground to practise afterwards. Got blisters of course.

Dec. 4th Wednesday
Were all given free passes over the South Australian Railways. Practised again and dined at the club in the evening. Went to the theatre afterwards to see "School" as we were all invited to be present. Went behind the scenes.

Dec. 5th Thursday
Stirling drove Mr. and Mrs. Hornby etc. and self from the "Crown and Sceptre" to a picnic at Mr. Scott's, the Mayor's, at Mount Lofty. He gave us a very good lunch after which we walked to the top of the hill and were rewarded for our pains with a very fine view. Mr. Scott's house is 12 miles from Adelaide and coming back is of course very much down hill. Stirling brought us back, 4 in hand, in 53 minutes. Dined at the club in the evening.

Dec. 6th Friday.
Mr. Parr drove MacKinnon and me to a place called Hackham 17$^1/_2$ miles off. Mac wanted to see a Mr. Allen, son of one of his father's tenants. He was very pleased to see us. On the way we had lunch, which we took with us, in an old man's garden named Cox, we had a long talk with him and he was quite delighted to see anybody from the Old Country. We got back to Adelaide about 6.45. Had dinner at the hotel. Some of the other fellows turned up late, so the landlady calmly refused to let them have any dinner. This did not, of course, wash. I need hardly say they got it. The above will give one an idea of hotel life, at present, in Adelaide.

Dec. 7th Saturday.
The Adelaide tramways were opened. Free passes were sent to all the team, and an invitation to the opening lunch. Harris, only, went; dined with Hornby at the "Crown and Sceptre". Mac and Webb also went, the rest dining at Government House.

Dec. 8th Sunday.
Mrs. Baker gave us a picnic to Morialta. Harte drove some of us over there in his drag, or rather to Brougham Place where me met. I then changed into Stirling's drag. We arrived at Morialta, a distance of about 8 miles and had a very pleasant lunch. Walked to a pretty waterfall, that is quite close, afterwards. Returned about 5.30 after spending a very pleasant day. Went to dine at Government House at 7.30. Boss did not go as he did not feel well.

Dec. 9th Monday.
Went up to Horn's place in the morning and watched some of our fellows play tennis. Lunched at the Club. Practised afterwards and dined at the club with Horn in the evening before going to the Assembly Ball which was given in our honour. I enjoyed myself very much. The room was very tastefully decorated. At the far end were placed bats and wickets and tents on each side where refreshments were served. Bye the bye I met Sandeman, an old BNC[7] man, very unexpectedly. He had just arrived from the Cape, so called on me at the hotel.

Dec. 10th Tuesday.
First day of our match v 18 South Australians.[8] In fact our first match in the Colonies. They went in first and made 110. Jarvis played best for them with 28. We got 106 for 4 wickets, Webbe 35, Hornby 42 not out.

Dec. 11th Wednesday.
Match continued. All our side out for 185. Self run out for 2. Hornby got 78. 10 of the 18 down in their 2nd innings for 98. Had to pack up after dining at the club in the evening.

Dec. 14th.
Went to breakfast with Fitzroy at the club. Match continued at 12.30. South Australians made 37 more, total 135.[9] Went in to get 63 lost 7 wickets in doing it. Self and Emmett not out with 20 and 5 respectively.

7. Brasenose College, Oxford.
8. The match began on December 12 and finished on December 14.
9. There are minor discrepancies throughout the Diary between Royle's figures and those in *Wisden*. In this instance, the South Australians made 137 and Emmett was 6 not out.

Dined at the club in the evening and left Adelaide afterwards for the Semaphore where we went on board the "Victorian" for Melbourne. Sailed about 12 o'clock at midnight. We had all spent a very pleasant time in Adelaide, being treated with the greatest hospitality. Was very sorry to leave.

Dec. 15th.
On the sea. Ill all day.

Dec. 16th.
Ill in the morning, but rather better. Arrived at Sandridge end of Port Phillip about 4 o'clock p.m. We passed the heads entering the bay about 12 o'clock. Queenscliffe is on the left on entering. The distance of this port from the heads to the landing place is 10 miles thus forming an immense harbour as the heads are only about 1 mile apart. Even when inside you very nearly lose sight of land. On arriving off Sandridge we were met by the committee and several gentlemen of the Melbourne Club, who had come out in a steam launch.We went on board and were landed at Sandridge. Heard of the death of Princess Alice.[10] Were driven to the Town Hall in drags and were there received by the Mayor, etc., who welcomed us to Melbourne and drank our healths in champagne. Went to see the end of the match between the Australians and 15 Victorians. The former won by about 5 wickets. Murdoch got 152. We all dined at the Melbourne Club with Blackwood in the evening except Maul who went to see his cousin who is Master of the Mint. Took up our quarters at the Oriental Hotel, Collins Street.

Dec. 17th.
Webbe and I went to lunch with Campbell at his father's house. Practised in the afternoon and went to Colonel Anderson's to play tennis afterwards. Dined with Robinson at South Yarra in the evening.

Dec. 18th
Played in a match v 18 West of England on the Melbourne ground.[11] Harris, Hornby, Lucas and Hone also played. We got 416. Hornby 27, Lucas 79, Hone 13, Harris 1 and self 8. Got the 18 out in 45 minutes

10. Queen's Victoria's second daughter (1843-78).

11. Not part of the official tour and not recorded in *Wisden*.

for 34 runs. Dined with Fanning at the club. A brother of Fred Fanning's who was at BNC with me.

Dec. 19th
Left cards on the Melbourne, Victoria and Athenaeum Clubs. Also on Croaker, Moore and Francis. Lunched at the hotel. Dined with Mr. Lloyd Jones and danced afterwards.

Dec. 20th
Infernal hot wind, dust flying about in clouds, heat very great. Went over the Mint with Mr. Broughton, the Master. Had very bad blisters, so did not practise. Walked round the town with Mrs. Hornby. Dined at the hotel and went to the Academy of Music in the evening, the vice-regal box being placed at our disposal. "Les Cloches de Corneville" was the piece. Mr. E. Trenchard called, when I heard for the first time of his father's death.

Dec. 21st.
Went with Lucas and Hone to St. Kilda before breakfast and had a splendid bath. Lunched at the club. Fanning drove me over to Yarra Bend, a short way from Melbourne where Webbe, Maul and I played for the Bohemians against that Club.[12] They won the toss and got 162. We got 62 for 4 wickets, Webbe 24, Maul 20, Self 9 not out. Drove back and dined with Mr. Francis in the evening.

Dec. 22nd.
Went over to St. Kilda and lunched with the Moores. Stayed there all day.

Dec. 23rd.
Bathed at St. Kilda. Practised in the afternoon and went to play lawn tennis at Lady Stawell's after. The house there had a narrow escape of being burnt down. The grass had caught fire round it and was put out just in time. Dined at the "Oriental" and went to the amateur theatricals at Glens in Collins St. after. They were very good, Mrs. Lewis, Miss Noel and Miss Burrup being especially prominent.

12. Neither this nor the game on December 24 were part of the tour programme.

Dec. 24th.
The twelve went over to Yarra Bend in the morning to play against 15 of the Melbourne Club. Harris won the toss and we stayed in the whole day making 434. Lucas 107, Webbe 58, Maul 45, Hornby and self 36, Harris 34, etc. Many of us got out on purpose. Dined at Government House (Sir George Bowen) in the evening. Met Major Pitt R.A. there who knew Arthur when in the 31st at Malta.

Dec. 25th.
Christmas Day. Went to church at St. Peter's. Had lunch at the hotel. Went to play lawn tennis at the Moores in the afternoon, returned to the "Oriental" for dinner when we drank the health of Old England. I drank the health and thought of all at home.

Dec. 26th.
Our first match in Melbourne commenced v 15 of Victoria. They won the toss and made 288 for 13 wickets. Our fielding not at all good. Campbell[13] played a very good innings for 128, nobody else getting 30.

Dec. 27th
Their innings terminated for 313. Lucas and Ulyett commenced for us. 1st wicket fell at 88. Kept them out the whole day, making 303 for 8 wickets. Lucas 90. Self 78, caught at square leg off a slow full pitch.

Dec. 28th.
Innings closed for 332 or 17 ahead. Got them out for 218. Match thus drawn. Dined at the club. All started by the 7 o'clock train for Colac to stay with the Robertsons. Special carriage on for us to Geelong where we changed and went on by special train. Met at Colac by Robertson and were driven to his place 10 miles off. Arrived about 12 o'clock had supper and went to bed being very tired.

Dec. 29th.
Slept very well. Walked down by a lake there was in front of the house. It was crowded with wild fowl and hundreds of wild black swan. The latter did not take any notice of us. Went up to the top of a hill close by and had splendid view. After lunch we went for a drive round the

13. Donald Campell had got a Blue at Oxford in 1874.

country etc. Very cold it was too. Roads did not appear to be any object whatever, as we drive right across country. Did not go to church as the *nearest* one is 10 miles off.

Dec. 30th.
Got up at 6.30 a.m. and drove with Fanning, Lucas and Schultz to shoot at Mr. Murray's place, 4 miles from Robertson's. Had plenty of walking over rocks etc. but could not get near the wild fowl. Saw plenty of wild geese, ducks, etc.etc. Returned to Robertson's for lunch. He had got down about 300 pigeons for our benefit, but after a short time, Lucas and I went ferretting rabbits and got about 30 in a very short time. Went to bed very early.

Dec. 31st.
Had to get up at 3.30 to catch the early train at Colac. Passed through Geelong and arrived at Melbourne about 10.30. Practised in the afternoon and dined at the club in the evening, the old university[14] dinner being on, to which we were invited. Went to ball at Mr. Francis' after.

Jan. 1st.
Drove to the champion races in a four in hand. Very hot day indeed. Dined at the hotel in the evening.

Jan. 2nd.
Our match v the Australian Eleven commenced.[15] We won the toss. Unluckily for us, rain fell. Lost 7 wickets for 26 runs. Absolom and Harris only getting double figures. The former 52, the latter 33. All out for 113. Got 3 of their best wickets for 37. Should have done very well had our fielding been better. Ulyett missed Spofforth, a very easy chance, directly he came in. No other wicket fell and at the end of the day's play they had got 95. Dined at the hotel in the evening.

Jan. 3rd.
Walker[16] and Penn arrived by the P & O Mail from England about 11.30 a.m. Match continued – they got 254. We lost 6 wickets for 103.

14. Oxford.
15. This match retrospectively was recognised as a Test match.
16. I.D. Walker, to whom the original invitation to tour Australia had been sent.

Light very bad. Shadows across the ground etc. Went to dine with Croaker at Burnley. Hone and MacKinnon also went. Went with the Croakers to see the Pantomime "Jack the Giant Killer" at the Theatre Royal afterwards. Received letters from home.

Jan. 4th.
Our last 4 wickets pulled the score up to 160, leaving the Australians 18 to get which they did without losing a wicket. Lucas, Hone and I went over to the Moores at St. Kilda in the afternoon and played tennis. Dined with Campbell at the Club, after dinner Hone and I went to the Riddles' dance at Elsternwick.

Jan. 5th.
Lunched at the Lewis' South Yarra, had supper at the Moores.

Jan. 6th.
Got up at 7 and went by the 8 o'clock train to St. Kilda. Breakfasted at the Moores, Lucas and Hone also went. Started from there afterwards to a picnic at Fern Tree Gully, given by Dr. Fitzgerald. The gully is 25 miles from Melbourne. Mr. and Mrs. Hornby drove in a buggy. Got there about 1 o'clock. The roads were very bad indeed. Went to the top of the gully and had a very fine view. On the road to the gully one of the coachmen was run over, but not seriously hurt. On returning from the top we had lunch. Just before we arrived Dr. Fitzgerald's servant cut his eye very badly through a soda water bottle bursting. Had a pleasant drive back, Lucas and I stayed for supper at the Moores and returned to Melbourne after.

Jan. 7th.
Left Melbourne for Tasmania per S.S. "Southern Cross" at 11 o'clock. A good many people were present to see us off. The smells going down the Yarra from the fellmongering establishments[17] are something fearful. The steamer was awfully crowded. When going up Port Phillip Bay there were heaps of porpoises to be seen, 3 or 4 kept just ahead of the steamer, this is very often to be seen. Arrived at Queenscliffe the head of the bay about 4 o'clock. Outside the heads it was luckily pretty smooth.

17. Where skins were prepared for tanning.

Jan. 8th.
Very fine night. Arrived off the Tasmanian heads at 8.30 a.m. and entered the river Tamar. The scenery up the river is very pretty, hills rising gradually on either side, covered with growth of different kinds from the native gum tree to the English hawthorn hedge, the first we had seen since leaving England. The distance from the heads to the Launceston the landing place is 45 miles. The pilot came on board about 11.40 and at 11.45 some of the Launceston Cricket Association. We reached the quay about 12 o'clock. It was a very hot day, but there was a nice cool breeze blowing. Were driven to the "Criterion" where, as usual, the Mayor proposed our health. Before lunch we went to the public baths, which belong to a quaint old curiosity-shop keeper. After lunch we went to see the cricket ground and were driven from there in a 4 in hand to the station in order to catch the 3 o'clock train for Hobart Town. It is a single line, 3ft 6ins wide and the curves on it are simply a caution, the end of the train in many cases being only a few yards from the engine. The train itself in some cases forms as it were the letter S. The distance to Hobart Town is 130 miles and it takes 6 hours to do this distance. We arrived at Hobart Town about 9-10 p.m. The platform was crowded, a 4 in hand was waiting for us, so we drove at once to the "Ship" where accommodation had been secured for us. After supper, being very tired, we went to bed at once.

Jan. 9th.
Wrote to my father per S.S. "Aconcagua" as I heard by chance she was to sail on Tuesday. Only had time to write a short letter. Our match commenced vs Southern Tasmania. We won the toss but put them in. All out for 82. We got 133. Hornby not out 61. It was a most beautiful day. Very funny ground for cricket, but beautifully situated. On the one side Mt. Wellington towers above the town and on the other is the River Derwent, Government House, etc. In the evening we went to the Hobart Town Assembly Ball which was given in our honour. Picked up a bracelet in the street whilst walking back.

Jan. 10th.
Match continued, got them all out for 142 and won by 6 wickets. Ball given to us at Government House in the evening by Governor Wells to which we nearly all went. I enjoyed it very much.

2. Lord Harris's English Team 1878–79.
Back row: F. Penn, A.J. Webbe, C.A. Absolom, S.S. Schultz, L. Hone.
Middle row: F.A. MacKinnon, A.N. Hornby, Lord Harris, H.C. Maul, G. Ulyett.
Front row: A.P. Lucas, V.P.F.A. Royle, T. Emmett.

3. Lord Harris as a young man.

4. A.N. Hornby.

5. George Ulyett.

6. The Australians who played against Lord Harris's English Team, Melbourne, January 2, 3 & 4, 1879.
Standing: J. Blackham, T. Horan, G.H. Bailey, J. Conway, A. Bannerman, C. Bannerman, W.L. Murdoch.
Seated: F.R. Spofforth, F. Allan, D.W. Gregory, W. Midwinter, T.W. Garrett, H.F. Boyle.
For the match, Bailey was replaced by T.J.D. Kelly.

51. Hornby was bowled by Spofforth also soon after for 67. Ulyett got 55 & Harris 41. Towards the end of the innings Spofforth cut up the wicket to such an extent with his feet that it was impossible to play. Evans pitched nearly every ball into the marks & the innings closed for 267. We got A. Bannerman & Thompson down for 51 runs. Went to see "John Bull" at the Royal with Lucas in the evening.

Match continued at 12 oclock. At lunch 3 wickets were down for 130, after lunch the wickets fell rapidly, all being out for 177, 90 behind our score. Murdoch played a splendid not out innings for 82. They followed on about 4 oclock, shortly afterwards Murdoch was given "run out" by "Coulthard" our Umpire, upon which a most disgraceful scene occurred. The "Larrikins" rushed the ground. Harris refused to change our Umpire, as we considered the decision a good one. Play was consequently stopped for the day, as the crowd would not let us go on. During the row, Harris was struck with a stick, but not hurt. It was a most disgraceful affair & took its origin from some of the "better" class in the Pavilion.

– L –

7. A page from Vernon Royle's diary.
Entries for February 7th and 8th, 1879.

8. The Melbourne Cricket Ground during a Grand Intercolonial Cricket Match, January 1st, 1864.

9. The Reverend Vernon Royle (1854–1929).
A portrait in oils painted by Oswald Birley in June 1907 and presented to the M.C.C. by J.E. Royle in 1930.

Jan. 11th
Got up at 7 a.m. and drove with Absolom to the Huon 25 miles off. Visited Fern Tree Gully on the way. The scenery all along was beautiful. Arrived at Victoria on the banks of the Huon about 1.10. Had lunch and looked about the place afterwards, not much to be seen. Started back about 3 o'clock. The roads were very hilly, one hill alone being $4^1/2$ miles long. The weather was very squally and we were caught several times in the rain. The drive back was bitterly cold. All dined at the Tasmanian Club in the evening as the members had invited us all to dine there. Found the owner of the bracelet, namely Mrs. Swann.

Jan. 12th.
Left Hobart Town for Launceston by special train at 12 o'clock. The ladies stayed behind, also MacKinnon, Webbe and Walker. There was a large crowd to see us off. It luckily rained just after we started so we were free at any rate from the dust. The line passes along the river Derwent, on which Hobart Town is built, for some way, the scenery is very pretty. Arrived at Launceston about 6.25 and walked to the Criterion Hotel. Dined at 7 o'clock and walked to see a waterfall called the Cataract a little distance out of the town, afterwards. We had rather a steep hill to climb which was very hard work after dinner.

Jan. 13th.
Began our match v 18 of N Tasmania at 10.45. We won the toss again but put them in. They only got 49. We got 212, Penn 53 highest scorer. Got 6 of their wickets down in the 2nd innings for 35. Major Cox, Mary Hayne's friend, played against us here. We drew wickets at 6.30 and as it was only a one day's match, we won easily. A dance was given to us at the Town Hall in the evening.

Jan. 14th
Left Launceston by the S.S. "Mangana" at 3.30 for Melbourne. Had a very smooth passage. Went over a tin smelting works before we left.

Jan. 15th.
Slept pretty well. About 10.00 a.m. when looking over the bows I saw a small shark, the first I ever saw. Arrived at the mouth of the Yarra going up to Melbourne about 2.45. Moored at the wharf about

4 o'clock p.m. Went to the hotel and dined with Blackwood at the club in the evening.

Jan. 16th.
Lucas, Mrs. Hornby and I went over to see the Moores in the afternoon. Stayed there for dinner.

Jan. 17th.
Left Melbourne for Sydney by the 3 o'clock train. Arrived at Euroa, where the bank was stuck up, a short time ago, by the Kellys, about 7 o'clock. Reached Banalla about 8 and shortly after leaving the latter place we were fortunate enough to see a bush fire by night. It is a splendid sight. The forest is in one mass of flame, the latter running up the trees like lightning. It extended for more than a mile along the line and further than we could see into the bush. It lit up the country as if it were day. On all the platforms along there were crowds of people, who stood staring into the windows of the saloon. We reached Wodonga the terminus of the Victorian Railway about 11 o'clock. Drove from there to Albury where we had to take coach for Wagga Wagga. On our way there we crossed the river Murray which divides Victoria from New South Wales. We put up at the "Globe", a very primitive sort of place indeed. It was quite full, or nearly so, and consequently many of us had to sleep out on the verandah. We had to leave again at 5 a.m. by coach for Wagga and as it was 3½ miles from Wodonga we had not much time for sleep, after we had had something to eat.

Jan. 18th.
Left the Globe Hotel, Albury for Wagga Wagga at 6.30 a.m. The distance is about 90 miles. The coach is a most curious looking thing. There are no windows, only curtains, the springs are made of leather and present a most comical appearance. Ordinary springs would not do for the bush roads at all. Soon after leaving we entered the bush and were in it till within a few miles of Wagga. The journey is very monotonous as there is no scenery worth seeing, from the time of leaving Albury till you get to Wagga, there is nothing to be seen but gum trees. The road is a mere track through the bush and it is marvellous to see how the drivers pick their way through the stumps of trees, etc. The dust was awful and the jolting worse. We changed horses about every 15 miles or so. We at length reached Wagga about

7.30 p.m. having been on the coach 13 hours. Very glad we were to get to the "Australian" Hotel and partake of a good dinner that was nearly ready when we arrived. I need hardly say there was a good deal of champagne knocking about which was very acceptable, our throats being choked with dust. The rooms were so hot that many slept on the balcony and were consequently eaten up by mosquitoes. Young Maul was bitten by bugs.

Jan. 19th
After breakfast Lucas and I went to see Ortons shop in Gerwood Street. It is now the surgery of a Doctor Wren. Went to St. John's Church at 11. The text was XI Luke and 15 verse. Wagga is a very dusty place. The streets are merely loose sand. We had dinner at 1.30. Left for the station 4 miles off at 4.30. Train left for Sydney at 5.40. A sleeping car was attached.

Jan. 20th.
Had a pleasant journey. Slept very well. Arrived at Sydney a little after 7 a.m. Raining hard. Met at the station by some of the Cricket Association. Were driven in a drag and 4 horses to the Exchange Hotel, Gresham Street, where we were very glad to get a wash, etc. and a good breakfast. It rained the whole day.

Jan. 21st
Horne, an Old Rossallian, called on me in the morning, 8 years since I last saw him. He came to lunch. Went to the ground to practise in the afternoon, were welcomed in the pavilion by the Cricket Association.

Jan. 22nd.
Wrote home to the mater, or rather posted my letter. It rained so hard that we were not able to practise. Absolom and I went to a dance at the Youngs, Kentville, North Annandale in the evening. The 'road' was so bad that at one time the cabby had to take one of the lamps out to look for it.

Jan. 23rd.
Drove over with Harris, etc. to Coogee Bay a very pretty place. Lunched with Mort at the Union Club and practised after. Dined at the hotel and went to see "Lost in London" at the Queen's Theatre afterwards.

Jan. 24th.
Began our match v New South Wales. 11 a side. Spofforth was unable to play as he had been thrown out of a cab the night before and cut his wrist. They won the toss but put us in. We got 248. Penn 56, Ulyett 51, Harris 50 were the principal scorers. They got 16 for no wickets. Went to the Theatre Royal in the evening.

Jan. 25th.
Match continued, got them all out for 240. 8 behind our score. There were a tremendous lot of chances missed, which if taken, would have reduced their score considerably.

Jan. 26th.
We hired two launches and steamed about the bay or rather harbour. Had a most enjoyable day. When anchored, a shark kept swimming round the vessel. Got back to the hotel about 7.15 in time for dinner.

Jan. 27th.
The great day of festivity in Sydney being the 92nd anniversary of its foundation. The Regatta is always held on this day. Our match continued, we got 217, 6 of us getting between 20 and 30. Self 29 not out. Put them in to get 226. Got 2 down for 83. Webbe and I dined with Smythe an old Exeter College[18] man, at the Union Club.

Jan. 28th.
Match resumed and finished. At lunch we had 5 down for 120. After lunch our fielding was atrocious, missing several chances. Lost by 5 wickets. C. Bannerman and Massie knocking off the runs. All dined with the Hon. James White at the Union Club in the evening. Lucas was seedy, so did not go.

Jan. 29th.
My birthday. Played 22 of the Army and Navy, without our professionals, at the barracks[19]. Had a very pleasant day. They went in and got 157. We got 164 for 5 wickets. Self 29 not out. We went in for hitting. Dined with Moseley at the Australian Club. Went with Lucas and Penn to the theatre after.

18. Oxford.
19. Not part of the tour.

Jan 30th.
Left Sydney at 9 o'clock for Bathurst. The scenery along the line is very fine. Part of the line ascends the Blue Mountains by means of what is called the Zig-Zag. The Zig-Zag on the Bathurst side is a wonderful piece of engineering. The engine draws and pushes the train up alternately We arrived at Bathurst about 5.45 and were met by a crowd of people. Drove to the Royal Hotel and were, as usual, welcomed there.

Jan. 31st.
Began our match v 18 of Bathurst. Got them out for 47. We got 227. Many got out on purpose. Were entertained at a ball in the evening.

Feb. 1st.
Rained all day, so the match was drawn very much in our favour. Left again for Sydney at 6 o'clock. 2 carriages being put on to a luggage train. Got to Sydney on the Sunday about 7.15 a.m., having been 14 hours on the journey.

Feb. 2nd.
Went to bed on arriving at the hotel. Polly's birthday, thought about her. Went to the Cathedral in the evening.

Feb. 3rd.
Lucas, Penn and I left Sydney by the 9.45 a.m. train to stay with Dr. Jenkins at Nepean Towers. On arriving at the station, Douglas Park, about 12 o'clock we were rather surprised to find nobody there to meet us. In a few minutes, however, young Jenkins rode up and was equally surprised to see us, as his father had understood Webbe to say we were not coming. He was very glad to see us, however, and rode home about 2 miles for a buggy. We walked on as far as the river Nepean, the scenery was very pretty. Jenkins met us there and drove us to his father's house. We had lunch first and then went out rabbit shooting, about 5 miles off. They were in great profusion, in two hours we shot over 80. We then returned to the Towers very well satisfied with our day's sport.

Feb. 4th.
Started from Nepean Towers about 11 o'clock for some wild fowl shooting at Sir William McArthur's place about 12 miles off. They

were in great quantities, but very hard to get near. We managed to get about 9 couples. We went up to the house to lunch and stayed nearly all afternoon, so did not have very much shooting. Got back to Dr. Jenkins' about 8.45, rather late for dinner. We enjoyed the day immensely. Young Jenkins has a small cricket ground nearly opposite the house. He was awfully keen about it and wanted us to practise at every opportunity.

Feb. 5th.
Penn and Jenkins went down to practise as usual. Lucas and I kept away. About 11 o'clock we started off, 5 of us, on horseback to hunt 'wallabys' young kangaroos. Miss Jenkins came with us. It is a wonderful sight to see how the horses pick their way at full gallop through the trees etc. in the bush. We did not see any wallabys, the scrub was so thick, we had one or two chases, however, and the dogs killed a couple or so. We enjoyed ourselves immensely, returned to the house for lunch about 2 o'clock. Left Nepean Towers about 3 o'clock to catch the Sydney train at 3.30, where we arrived about 6.00. We were very sorry our visit was over, as we had enjoyed ourselves immensely. On our return to Sydney we found that the rest of the team had been (on) a trip up the Hawkesbury river during our absence, and much pleased they seemed to be with it. After dining at the Hotel we went to a ball on board the "Wolverene", given to us by the officers, etc. It was very well done, the ship being most tastefully decorated. There were nearly 480 people present so dancing was rather difficult. It passed off very well.

Feb. 6th.
Went to practise in the afternoon, dined with Penn at the Union Club afterwards and went to see "The Bells" at the Theatre Royal after. Bye the bye, the management of the theatres were most courteous as they sent us invitations to go whenever we liked.

Feb. 7th.
First day of our return match v 11 of New South Wales. Harris won the toss and sent Hornby and Lucas in about 12.10. They played magnificently, scoring 125 before they were parted. Lucas was bowled by Spofforth for 51. Hornby was bowled by Spofforth also soon after for 67. Ulyett got 55 and Harris 41. Towards the end of the innings

Spofforth cut up the wicket to such an extent with his feet that it was impossible to play. Evans pitched nearly every ball into the marks and the innings closed for 267. We got A. Bannerman and Thompson down for 51 runs. Went to see "John Bull" at the Royal with Lucas in the evening.

Feb. 8th.
Match continued at 12 o'clock. At lunch 3 wickets were down for 130. After lunch the wickets fell rapidly, all being out for 177, 90 behind our score. Murdoch played a splendid not out innings for 82. They followed on about 4 o'clock, shortly afterwards Murdoch was given "run out" by Coulthard our umpire, upon which a most disgraceful scene occurred. The "Larrikins" rushed the ground. Harris refused to change our umpire, as we considered the decision a good one. Play was consequently stopped for the day, as the crowd would not let us go on. During the row, Harris was struck with a stick, but not hurt. It was a most disgraceful affair and took its origin from some of the "better" class in the Pavilion.[20]

Feb. 9th.
Went to lunch with the Youngs at Annandale, returned to the Hotel for dinner.

Feb. 10th.
Match continued. Got them all out for 49, last 5 wickets going for no runs. Won the match in an innings and 41. Hornby caught C. Bannerman at mid off, low down with the left hand, a splendid catch. After the match Lucas, Penn, Schultz, Maul and I went out for a row. As we passed the "Wolverene", the blue jackets gave us 3 hearty cheers. We went on as far as Woolloomooloo Bay and then returned to the "Wolverene" where we found all the rest of our fellows. We had great fun. In the evening Commodore Wilson and some of the other officers dined with us at the Hotel. Webbe was great fun after, so was Captain Bruce of the "Cormorant" etc., etc., etc.

20. Harris was convinced that betting had been the root cause of the trouble. As a consequence of this no representative match was included in the programme for the visit of the Australians in 1880 though one was eventually arranged and took place at the Oval.

Feb. 11th.
Hornby, Webbe, Lucas, Schultz, Maul and I went out in Mr. Jackson's yacht, who had lent it to Symonds of the "Wolverene".We sailed all over the harbour and had great fun. At Manly beach we had lunch. I and one of the other officers going on shore where we got some oysters etc. The latter are in great profusion, nearly all the rocks being covered with them. It was too much trouble to gather them ourselves, so we bought a great bag full for 2 shillings. We returned about 6 o'clock. After packing up, as we had to leave for Melbourne in the evening, we dined with Mr. Dangar at the Union Club. Harris, Absolom, MacKinnon and Lucas did not go as they had started off overland. We left the club about 11.15 to catch the "Ly-ee-moon" which was to start from the wharf for Melbourne at 12 o'clock. Most of the fellows, dining with us, came to see us off, including some of the officers and blue jackets of the men-of-war then in harbour, *viz* "Wolverene", "Sapphire" and "Cormorant". They gave us three cheers as we left which we returned; as we passed the "Wolverene" we gave them three hearty cheers. She was lying some way off, but they heard them and gave us a hearty response. I turned in shortly after, the night was very dark.

Feb. 12th.
Ill just after my bath. Spent most of the day in my berth. Dr. Slade, the Spiritualist, is on board. A little better now 8.45 p.m. Sea going down.

Feb. 13th.
Slept pretty well, sea smooth, but wind very cold. Several of the people on board tried, in vain, to get a seance out of Dr. Slade. He, of course, refused. Passed Wilson's promontory, the most southern point of Australia, about 5 p.m. It was so close one could almost have thrown a stone on shore. Saw a seal close by here. There was a betting man on board named Thompson, a great cad, but very amusing.

Feb. 14th.
Arrived at the wharf Sandridge about 6.30 a.m. Left for the Oriental at 7.30. We were very lucky in having such a smooth passage. Practised in the afternoon.

Feb. 15th.
Harris, Absolom, MacKinnon and Lucas arrived at the hotel about 9 a.m. They came overland from Sydney. Had some first rate kangaroo hunting on the way. MacKinnon was in great form, I believe, in showing the others the way over their fences. I went over to St. Kilda to see the Moores in the afternoon.

Feb. 16th.
Drove with Mr. and Mrs. Hornby over to Melton, 25 miles off, to see the uncle of his father's gamekeeper, Parkinson by name, We started at 11 o'clock. Had a very pleasant though uninteresting drive. The old fellow was very much pleased to see us. Got back to Melbourne in time for dinner.

Feb. 17th.
Went over to play against 15 Bohemians at Yarra Bend, without our professionals. They won the toss and got 228. We got 97 for 1 wicket. In the afternoon Penn unfortunately put his knee out when fielding a ball at long leg. Went to a dance at the Broughtons at the Mint in the evening.

Feb. 18th.
Match continued, all out for 255. I got 21 not out. Penn could not play. Had to field out all afternoon. They got 260 for 13 wickets. Another accident befell us, as Lucas split his fingers between, when catching a ball. The Melbourne Club gave us a dinner in the evening. I enjoyed it very much.

Feb. 19th.
Went to play tennis at the Cornishs' with Webbe in the afternoon, over at Toorak. Dined with Blackwood, who lives close by, afterwards. Webbe remained all night but I returned with Lord and Lady Harris.

Feb. 20th.
Hot wind blowing. Went to practise in the afternoon. Lucas and I went over to play lawn tennis at St. Kilda afterwards. Mr. and Mrs. Hornby and Miss Ingram came later on. We all dined there and got back to Melbourne about 12.

Feb. 21st.
Wrote home to my father. 1st day of match v 11 of Victoria. We won the toss and got 325 of which Ulyett got 71, Hornby 50, Emmett 41, Harris 26, Lucas 38 and self 57. Got one of their wickets down for 2 runs. At the end of our innings the light was very bad. Went to dine with Mr. Pattinson at Scotts Hotel in the evening.

Feb. 22nd.
Mails leave for England per S.S. "Siam". Match continued. They got 261, 64 behind our score. We lost 3 wickets, Lucas, Hornby and Harris, for 59. Dined with Croaker in the evening.

Feb. 23rd.
Went with Mrs. Hornby to St. Peters, wretched service. Lunched with Mr. Lewis at South Yarra and walked over to supper at the Moores, St. Kilda, in the evening.

Feb. 24th.
Match continued. We got 171 leaving them 236 to get. They got 171 for 7 wickets.

Feb. 25th.
Match continued. Beaten by 2 wickets owing to our bad fielding. Most of the team left for Sandhurst in the evening. Absolom, Lucas and I remained behind.

Feb. 26th.
Got up in time to catch the 6.45 a.m. train for Sandhurst. Arrived there about 11. Went to the City Family Hotel where we were to stay. Commenced our match v 22 of Bendigo a little after 11. They won the toss and made 141. The dust was a fearful nuisance, we had to stop playing once or twice as it was impossible to see. Hornby and MacKinnon went in first and at 6 o'clock had made 138. Hornby not out 77. Mac not out 45. Went to Leon's Circus in the evening. The clown imitated Hornby batting. It was very amusing.

Feb. 27th.
Match continued. Hornby made 104. We were all out for 304. A good many of us did not try to play as we were not in want of more runs.

They had to make 164 to save the innings defeat. At 6.30 they had 3 runs to get and one wicket to fall. The match was thus *drawn.* Lucas, Maul, Hone, Mac and I returned to Melbourne by the 7.20 train. All round Sandhurst can be seen the remains of the gold digging. The country is dug out in sections, as it were, completely honeycombed. There is no digging going on there now.

Feb. 28th.
Spent the day in Melbourne, went to the theatre in the evening.

March 1st.
Left by 6.30 a.m. train for Ballarat and arrived about 10.30. It is a very nice little place and was at one time the centre of the gold country. There is mining going on there still, but the gold is not found now as it used to be in such quantities, i.e. on the surface. Our match v 22 of Ballarat was commenced shortly after 11 o'clock. We won the toss and made 304. Hornby 86. Harris 89. Webb 52. I only got 9, bowled by an underhand slow which unfortunately shot.

March 2nd.
Drove over with Campbell, MacKinnon and Hone to see the former's sister, Lady Wilson, who lived at Ercildoune[21] about 20 miles from Ballarat. It is a very pretty place indeed. Arrived there in time for dinner. In the afternoon walked to and ascended a hill called "The Peak". The view was very extensive and well worth seeing. Stayed at Lady Wilson's all night.

March 3rd.
Left in time to catch the train, about 5 miles off, at 9.47. Got back to Ballarat in time to continue match about 11. They only made 140, they had to follow on and were all out for 123. The match thus ended in our favour by an innings and 40 odd runs. Some of us returned to Melbourne in the evening.

March 4th.
Went with Lucas to play lawn tennis at St. Kilda. Stayed at the Moores to dinner and went with them to the Theatre Royal in the evening. "Queen's Evidence" was the piece.

21. This was an Estate.

March 5th.
Went to a picnic to Sunbury at Mr. Clarke's place. A special train left Melbourne about 11.40. We all went. There were a good many people there and I enjoyed it very much. Mr. Francis who has a house close by gave a small dance in the evening. Returned by special train to Melbourne at 11.30, after spending a very enjoyable afternoon and evening.

March 6th.
Went in Larnack's drag to the Melbourne Races. It was a miserably cold, dusty day. One of the jockeys named Watty Boyd was killed, poor fellow! The horse rolled over him. He was fearfully smashed about. Saw him carried in. He died about an hour after. His horse fell over a fallen hurdle. Dined at the hotel.

March 7th.
Return match v 11 of Victoria commenced. We won the toss again and got 248. Harris 67. Ulyett 47. Webbe 24 and self 75. They lost 6 wickets for 110. Dined at Judge Noel's in the evening and went to the theatre after.

March 8th.
The Victorians all out for 146. Followed their innings and made 155. We lost 4 wickets for 31. 54 being required to win. The light was very bad.

March 9th.
Went over to Brighton and lunched with Finlay Campbell. Returned to South Yarra in the evening and had supper at Mr. Agnew's.

March 10th.
The match v Victoria continued, which we won by 6 wickets.[22] Webbe and Lucas, the two not outs, getting the 23 required to win. We all dined together at the Hotel, several guests being asked. Harris presented Loughman, the M.C.C.[23] representative, who had gone about with us, with a ring on behalf of the team. It was a very handsome one. Hornby gave Harris a cigarette case, solid silver, on behalf of the team, etc. We had great fun after dinner, in the sitting room. Mr. Maul and Mr. B....n edifying the company with some acrobatic performances, etc.

22. This was the last official match of the tour.
23. Melbourne Cricket Club.

March 11th.
All the team, ladies as well, except Lucas, Penn and myself, left Melbourne for a trip to New Zealand in the S.S. "Albion". I dined at the Wilkies in the evening.

March 12th.
Lucas and Penn played against an 18 on the Melbourne ground for the Club. Neither of them got any runs. Lucas and I went to dine at the Moores, before going to a dance at Mr.Blackwood's.

March 13th.
We all 3 played for the Melbourne Club v a local 18. We got 137, of which I got 34. The other side got 197 and thus won the match. We went in a 2nd time, Penn and I going first, I got 19 when I got out and Lucas went in. In three quarters of an hour, we made 120. At six o'clock the score was about 160 for 2 wickets. Penn got about 70 and Lucas 59 or so not out. I dined with the Lewis's at South Yarra in the evening.

March 14th.
Lucas and I lunched with Mr. Blackwood, Little Collins Street, after leaving, Penn joined us when we went for a stroll, Bunny and I dined at the Riddels, Elsternwick and danced afterwards.

March 15th.
Arnold came to lunch with us at the hotel. Lucas and I went over to St. Kilda and played tennis at the Moores. Stayed there to dinner. Penn and Walker went to stay at Glenormiston.

March 16th.
Lunched at Judge Noel's, had a very nice walk in the afternoon, returned and went to supper at the Agnews.

March 17th.
St. Patrick's Day. A long procession passed up Collins St. and in front of the hotel about 12 o'clock, they were all decorated with green sashes. We lunched at the hotel and went over with Donald Campbell to Colonel Anderson's where we played lawn tennis. The Melbourne Liedertofell was on in the evening and as they had kindly given us tickets, Lucas and I took advantage of them and went. We enjoyed the singing etc. very much.

March 18th.
Raining hard. The first wet day we have had for a long time. It cleared off however before lunch, so I went over to lunch, according to promise, at Mrs. Agnew's, South Yarra. We afterwards walked over to Colonel Anderson's and played tennis. There were a good many there. From there I went to dine at the Moores.

March 19th.
Walked over to the Botanical Gardens. They are very pretty indeed and well worth seeing.In the afternoon we went over to the Moores. We left there about six as we had to return to Melbourne to dress as we were to dine with Robinson at South Yarra. Dr. Ford called for us a little after 7. We drove out and had a very jovial evening.

March 20th.
Went down into the town. Met Loughman who returned with us to lunch.Had to pack up all heavy baggage to go to Sydney, en route for *home.* Went through the Museum, Public Library and Art Gallery. They were well worth seeing. Dined at Judge Noel's and went with them to the theatre.

March 21st.
Went to lunch at the Wilkies. As I had to get shells, etc. for some of our fellows who were in New Zealand, I wrote to a man named Warrington, Manley Beach, Sydney, to have some ready for me by the time we arrived.Went to a dance at Mr. Burny's, St. Kilda. Penn returned from Glenormiston (Finlay's place).

March 22nd.
A very beautiful day. Lunched early, 12.30, and then went to Williamstown to see Harry Maul off by the "Assam" for England. Emmett and Ulyett went too.[24] She left about 2.20. We dined at the hotel and went to see George Geith after.

March.23rd.
Lunched at Judge Noel's and returned to supper at the Wilkies, Collins St. in the evening.

24. There seems to be some inconsistency in who went to New Zealand on March 11. Royle, Lucas and Penn briefly visited the colony on April 1.

March 24th
Left cards etc. on Melbourne Club etc. etc. Went to say good-bye to the Moores, etc. Croaker, Loughman etc. asked us to lunch at the club at 1 o'clock, and as we had to leave for Sydney at 2.55 we had not much time, what with packing, etc. They all came to see us off at the station. We at length reached Wodonga, the terminus of Victorian Railways, took bus to Albury, 4 miles off, and caught the coach 12.30 a.m. for Wagga Wagga nearly 90 miles off.

March 25th.
After a very tedious journey overland, we reached Wagga Wagga about 2.30 p.m. Had lunch at the Criterion Hotel and then drove to the station 4 miles off, in time to catch the 5.50 train for Sydney. We were lucky enough to get a sleeping car and slept very well.

March 26th.
Arrived at Sydney about 7. a.m. Drove to the Union Club where we got rooms. Very glad we were to have a good wash etc. after which we enjoyed our breakfast immensely. We got our passage tickets etc. from Gilchrist & Co. Bought the shells I had written about and also some photos etc. In the afternoon went on board the "Australia" to see our berths etc. Had a good dinner at the club and went to see "Neck or Nothing" at the Theatre Royal. Lunched with Hone.

March 27th.
After lunching at the club we started for the quay. We there went on board the "Herald" which took us all off to the "Australia". The latter was lying out at anchor in the harbour. We ought to have started at 3 o'clock but it was after 5 before we got under weigh owing to the mails being late. There were a great number of small boats and steamers to see *us* off or rather some particular individual named Hudson belonging to some firm in Sydney. All the hands were there. Dr. Slade the Spiritualist was on board, on his way to San Francisco. We soon got outside the Heads, there was a heavy swell on, and we rolled considerably. I managed however to do full justice to dinner, after which I retired to my berth and slept very well.

March 28th.
Felt pretty well before sitting down to breakfast but alas! the feeling did not last long. I had to disappear and kept up my reputation as a first rate sailor. I reached the haven in safety and parted with what little I had managed to eat. Felt much better after and was well for the rest of the day. A very cold wind and sea still lumpy. Enjoyed my dinner in the evening immensely.

March 29th.
Still a heavy roll, feeling quite well however for a wonder. Sun very hot. Got my face very much blistered.

March 30th.
Very nasty morning. Raining hard. Had service in the morning and a collection for the seamen's orphan fund. A man named Chalmers, a missionary officiated. We had no prayers. 5 hymns, very badly sung, etc., etc. In the evening he gave us a long discourse on the growth of mission work in the South Pacific Islands and the intended mission to be undertaken in New Guinea. He spoke very well but was rather monotonous.

March 31st.
Passed Three Kings Islands on the port side about 6.30 a.m. Sighted New Zealand about 8.15. Very hazy morning. Passed Spirits Bay North Coast about 9.15. The latter is so called because the natives imagine that the spirits of the dead congregate there before flitting out to sea. We passed the North Head soon after, the sea having gone down considerably. Expect to arrive at Auckland about 2 a.m. Bitterly cold all day. Saw some very large flying fish, the largest, by far, I have yet seen. They very much resemble mackerel in colour. Going along in fine style.

April 1st.
Arrived at the wharf Auckland at 3.15 a.m. Got up early and went ashore before breakfast. Could not find where our fellows were staying. Returned on board to breakfast. The bay and surroundings are very pretty, but there is nothing worth seeing in Auckland itself. We ought to have left at 2.00 p.m. but were kept again, the mails being late, till 7.45. Harris, the ladies, etc. and all the rest joined us here and very

glad we were to see them again.[25] We did not consider however that His Lordship and Hone were improved by the wretched stubble that adorned their chins. They were all looking very well. The Maoris (natives of New Zealand) are a curious looking race. Their faces are tattooed to a great extent. They are however a fine, powerful race of men. There are very few in Auckland but are still in great numbers up country. It was a beautiful moonlight night when we steamed up the harbour.

April 2nd.
Met an old schoolfellow named Armstrong on board, on his way home, after travelling over Australia, etc., for about 8 months. Webbe is in the same cabin with me. We had a very good night's rest as it was luckily smooth. In fact so far, i.e. from Sydney, we have been very lucky.

April 3rd.
Rough night, strong head winds. Scarcely a dry spot on board. We are to have two Thursdays running in order to make the time right, as in going East round the world a day is gained.

April 4th
Sea very much calmer, still a head wind. Entered the Tropics, i.e. 23° N & S of the Equator. Ship rolling a great deal. One of the stewards was caught by Anderson in his cabin, with his hand in one of his pockets, evidently intent on stealing. He was reported, and set to work in the stoke hole. Afterwards put in irons, because he would not work.

April 5th.
False alarm of fire, to see if men were ready for their stations, etc. It was very well done. The ladies on board were all told of it beforehand. Saw a very fine lunar rainbow at 7.15 p.m. In the evening the stewards of the ship gave a nigger entertainment.

April 6th.
Very nice day indeed. Sighted the Navigator Islands about 3 o'clock, but were not fortunate enough to reach them before dark (6.15 p.m.).

25. Harris and some of the party had played a match in Canterbury which was drawn.

The sun went down about 5.45 and as the twilight is very short, it was dark directly. What little we saw of them, seemed to be very pretty. Had we been a little earlier, we should have stopped for a few minutes.

April 7th.
Weather getting much hotter. Heavy rain squall just after dinner, sea and wind rising.

April 8th.
Nothing particular happened today, still the same routine of ship life.

April 9th.
Beautiful day, close to the Equator. In the evening, a beautiful starlight night, saw the Great Bear and Southern Cross both at the same time about 10 p.m.

April 10th.
Wind rising very much. Sea ditto. Much cooler in consequence.

April 11th.
Sea and wind much the same. In the evening they both increased very much. Dr. Slade was very ill, his right side being paralysed.

April 12th.
Still strong head winds and sea very rough.

April 13th.
Very rough all day.

April 14th.
Sea and wind gone down considerably. Only 248 miles to Honolulu. Expect to get there about 11 tomorrow.

April 15th.
Sighted Oahu, one of the Sandwich Islands about 7.45 when we got up. Arrived off the Quay Honolulu about 10.30 a.m. Before arriving at the Quay about 50 of the native boys came around the ship, diving for money thrown overboard by the passengers. They swim like ducks. We landed a little after 11. It is a very pretty place, quite tropical of course. There is an old crater just above the town, called the Punch Bowl.

Penn, Lucas and I climbed up this before returning to the ship to lunch. We had a very fine view. After lunch we got 3 horses and rode about 7 miles to a place called the "Pali", the sight of the place. All the rest of our fellows and many of the passengers went. It was a beautiful view and well worth the trouble. The grandeur of the scenery burst out all at once, after coming out of a narrow gorge, we were on the brink of the precipice. The highest is about 2,000 feet high but we had not time to climb to the top of it. At our feet was stretched out beautiful great patches of vegetation and far away on the left, cliffs, perpendicular, rising to a height of 2,000 feet or more. These presented a grand appearance as the sun was shining on them and many different hues etc. were produced. Straight ahead and to the right, the sea opened out, looking very picturesque. We returned to Honolulu and arrived there about 4.30. There is a King of Honolulu and the Queen was just going to start (at 5 o'clock) for one of the other islands. We went down to the wharf so as to get a look at the pair of them. The natives are all civilised, the King was dressed in a white suit and looked very well. At six o'clock we returned to the "Australia" for dinner and as there was to be some dancing by the natives in the evening, we all returned to the Hawahan Hotel where it was to come off. We were sold however as it was a false report. There were two of Her Majesty's men of war in port, viz the "Triumph" and the "Opal" under Admiral de Horsey's flag. We did not meet any of the officers. I arrived back on board about 9 and as I was very tired, I turned in. We left the wharf for San Francisco about 12 at midnight.

April 16th.
When I awoke, I found the sea was running pretty high and a strong head wind blowing. This continued all day.

April 17th.
Strong head wind still blowing, sea not quite so high. About 4.20 in the afternoon one of the valves in the engine room broke, the consequence was we had to heave to for about 1$^{1}/_{2}$ hours. During this time we had great fun, catching some large birds, something like Molly Hawks, a species of albatross. These birds had been following us for some time and as soon as we stopped congregated at the stern of the ship in great numbers. There were about 5 or 6 lines out in no time, baited with

meat, etc. They rushed at it directly. We caught about 8 in a very short time. Their beaks are curved at the end and overhang a great deal, the hooks catch in the overhanging part and so the birds are caught. They measured one of them across the wings from tip to tip and it was 7ft 4ins. This was by no means the biggest we caught. Sometimes they only got hold of the meat and were so ravenous that they would not let go, till they were pulled in to a few feet of the deck.

April 18th.
Beautiful day, wind gone down and sea quite smooth. Very short run today, partly owing to the stoppage yesterday. In the evening some of the passengers gave a nigger entertainment. It passed off very well indeed.

April 19th.
Rolling again a great deal. One of the chains connecting the steam steering apparatus broke, we ran about 5 or 6 miles out of our course in no time, as the ordinary wheel was not in good order. Bye the bye there was rather a joke on board this morning. Last evening after the performance was over, an old gentleman named Rae thanked the performers for the trouble and care they had taken to entertain us and during his speech said "down with the rag" referring to a small flag one of the "niggers" was carrying for stage purposes. This happened to be the American ensign. This morning two of the many Americans on board asked him what he meant by insulting their flag. Such rubbish. The old fellow was quite taken aback, not knowing to what they referred. He, however, pacified them by saying it was a common thing in any theatre to hear the expression in reference to the Union Jack. The above shows how thin skinned some of the Americans are. I, for my part, never noticed the expression at all. Heavy rain squall just passed over the ship 3.45.

April 20th.
A very cold day. Had service as usual in the saloon. Mr. Seddons officiated. I am afraid his best friend could not say he was a success. He styles himself a lay reader. I never heard the service so mutilated in my life. In the Litany, after the prayer for our most Gracious Majesty, he popped in, when we were in the middle of the response, with "and

the President of the United States". I suppose this was to appease the wounded feelings of the Americans who were so much annoyed at what I related above. Wrote home to my father.

April 21st
Fine weather still continues. The Chief Engineer took several of us down to see the engine room. It was very well worth seeing. In the evening some Amateur Theatricals took place. They passed off very well indeed. The two pieces selected, were "A Bilious Attack" and "Little Toddlekins". Lord Harris took the principal characters in each. I acted as prompter to the second piece.

April 22nd.
Bitterly cold day, wind and sea rising. Had to look up all my things preparatory to packing up. Lady Harris kindly took my book with the cricket accounts in to paint the different ribbons over the portraits of the team, etc.

April 23rd.
Wind blowing rather hard, sea rough, very cold. Sighted land about 4.15. Pilot came on board about 5.35. Very misty, could not see the Farrell Lone Islands about 4 o'clock, as it was so misty. Arrived at the Golden Gate at 6.30 p.m., the Seal Islands and Cliff House being on the right. Could not see very much as it was unfortunately getting dark. Steamed up the Harbour, which seemed very pretty and cast anchor opposite the town. As soon as we cast anchor, the steamer was boarded by any amount of agents etc. for hotels, railways, etc. Mail went off immediately. Did not go ashore.

April 24th.
Just before 8.30 the "Australia" was taken alongside the wharf, the customs officers luckily passed our baggage etc. without examination, so after a little delay we found ourselves in most luxurious quarters at the Palace Hotel. The latter is a most magnificent pile of buildings, made of wood. 1015 beds can be made up. There is a large courtyard, as it were, on entering which is lighted by the electric light. The different storeys look down into this, corridors being all round. Took tickets by Quincy RR for New York.

April 25th.
Went to see round the town etc. Had a little practice in the afternoon. Harris, Absolom, MacKinnon, etc., left for Yosemite Valley in the afternoon. They have a peculiar kind of train car which runs up and down the steepest part of the city. It is worked by means of a wire rope which revolves, at the bottom of the cars a 'clip' is fixed which can be attached or detached by the driver, to the above rope. It has a very peculiar appearance.

April 26th.
The prices in America seem to be very high. A dollar for this, a dollar for that, money soon goes. At 7 o'clock we left the hotel to catch the 8 o'clock train. We had to cross the ferry to Oakland. At length we arrived at the station, our luggage checked etc. Managed to make ourselves at home in a Pullman's car. We started soon after and arrived at a place called Lathrop about 12.30 where we stayed 20 minutes for lunch. We reached Sacramento about 2.45 and the foot of the Sierra Nevada about sunset. The scenery here is very beautiful, unfortunately it was soon dark so we had not an opportunity of seeing much. It was just sufficiently light at 7 o'clock when we arrived at Cape Horn to see the beauties of the latter. You can stand on the platforms of the cars and look right over the side of the mountain to a great depth. It was a most imposing sight. The highest point reached by the railway is called the Summit, about 7,000 feet above sea level. The snow looked very beautiful by moonlight. Near the top snow sheds are built, in some places these are joined on to the side of the mountain, so that the snow slips over the top, when it slides down the mountain and is precipitated in the abyss below. Others of the sheds are merely diamond shaped. These sheds extend for a distance of 45 miles. Slept very well.

April 27th.
The scenery had very much altered when I awoke, the beautiful scenery of the grand Nevada range had given place to the trackless prairie, most desolate in appearance. Had breakfast at a place called Humboldt. There were some of the native Indians here of the "Pinte" (?) Race, they appeared quite civilized. The women carried their children on a board, slung over their backs. The children were strapped to this with their legs extended out quite straight, they could

not possibly move, their arms only being free and even this was not so in some cases. At the head part of the board there was a wicker work shade attached to keep off the sun. On through the prairie to Winnemma at 10.45 and Battle Mountain at 1.15 where we had lunch, or rather some of the others had. I did not partake as the charge was 2 dollars, at least so they told me. Passed over Whirlwind Valley and arrived at Beowawe about 2.55. As one passes through the former, little whirlwinds of sand can be seen in all directions, some rising to a height of 30 feet or more, hence its name. At Palisades the dull monotony of the prairies is varied a little by the rugged and lofty crags on each side the line; arrived at Wells a little after 8 p.m.

April 28th.
The prairie for the most part is covered with a little bush which is called sage brush. Have left the rocks etc. of the Palisades and are again in the prairie. In the distance every now and then the tops of the mountains could be seen clad with snow. Left Corinne about 7 a.m. and crossed the Bear River shortly after. At 8 o'clock we arrived at Ogden where we had breakfast. Ogden is the junction for Salt Lake City, Utah, about 2 hours in the train. Webbe, Hone and Anderson left us here, in order to pay it a visit. Soon after leaving Ogden, we passed the Devil's Slide, two natural walls of rocks running down the face of the mountain about 10 yards apart or not quite so much, and Pulpit Rock shortly after. It was here where Brigham Young preached to his followers on his first arrival. It is on the left of the line on leaving Ogden for Omaha. The scenery here is very grand. Lofty precipices on the left of the line and mountains gradually descending on the right. Stayed at Evanston for lunch at 2.30 and at Green River for supper at 8.40. We have been in the Rocky Mountains for some time, but with the exception of what I have mentioned above, the scenery is very disappointing. Why they are called the 'Rocky' Mountains it is impossible to make out. The height is certainly very great, as the rail track runs at the height of 6,000 feet above the sea level.

April 29th.
Arrived at Rock Creek about 8.40 a.m. We had breakfast here. Shortly after leaving we entered upon the country where antelopes, elk, etc. abound. We had the satisfaction of seeing 2 or 3 herds of the former,

not far away on the right. It was a very pretty sight, to see them sweep away up over the brow of the hill. Arrived at Cheyenne about 2 where dinner was prepared. We had ours in the carriage, much cheaper etc. We had brought a basket with us from "Frisco". We stayed at Ledray in the evening for supper. We had ours in the carriage again. There was a great deal of lightning in the evening. I never saw anything like it before. It lit up the whole sky. It was marvellously vivid.

April 30th.
There was a great deal of rain in the night. Stayed at Grand Island for breakfast. Reached Omaha about 4 o'clock and left soon after, crossing the Missouri to Council Bluffs, where we had to change from the Central Pacific Railway by which we had been travelling, into the Burlington and Quincy Line. An eating car was attached to the train here for the first time. We left shortly after 5 and had a very good dinner, whilst on the way, for 75 cents i.e. about 3 shillings. Went much faster on this line, saw many wild-fowl shortly after leaving Council Bluffs. The Missouri, where we crossed it, was not at all an imposing river, the water was very dirty and muddy, no doubt this was owing to the snow water, coming down.

May 1st.
Slept first rate and had a very good breakfast in the car, on getting up. Arrived at Chicago about 3.40 p.m. We had decided to stay a day here, so drove to the Grand Pacific Hotel. The latter is a very large building, but not equal to the "Palace" at Frisco. Walked about the town till dinner at 6.40. There are some very fine streets here, it is amazing to think the town as it now stands could have been burnt down such a short time ago (about '71). Went to see Edwin Booth as Richelieu at McVicker's Theatre in the evening. He is the brother of Wilkes Booth, murderer of President Lincoln. He was himself shot at a few nights before we arrived. Liked Chicago very much.

May 2nd.
Directly after breakfast we started off to see the Stock Yards, a little way out of the town. It is a wonderful sight. About 12,000 pigs are killed here in a day, when the full number of hands are working. The wretched pig is slung up by one man, by machinery worked by steam, it is then passed on to another, who sticks it, passed on from there into

boiling water and appears at the other end flayed etc., this does not take above 3 minutes. They got through an immense quantity whilst we were there. It is very curious to see them kill bullocks too. They drive two or three into a narrow box, a man there stands above them with a long iron rod, with this he takes a shot at the poor animal's neck. The latter drops directly, the spinal cord being severed. The working day is from 7 a.m. on till 5.30 with 1/2 hour for dinner. This leaves only 10 hours for work in which the enormous number of 12,000 is killed. Returned to the hotel for lunch and left in time to catch the 5.15 train for Niagara. Hone, Webbe and Anderson arrived just before we left. Had dinner in the train.

May 3rd.
Passed Detroit in the night. The train here passes over the River St. Clair in boats. It is very annoying we did not see the river by day as I believe it is very pretty. Arrived at London about breakfast time. Hornby met an old friend named Patterson, he knew him when out here in 1872. On arriving at Niagara about 1.40 we took traps and drove to the Prospect House Hotel. The latter is situated right above the Falls on the Canadian side. To describe one's first sight of the Falls is impossible. They are simply marvellous. The American Fall is the higher of the two but the Canadian is the grandest. The volume of water is immense. The former is about [?] feet high and about 900 feet across. This is on the opposite side as one drives from the station and is the first that bursts upon the view. Before arriving at the above there is a very elegant suspension bridge, the view of the falls from here is grand. Between the American and the Canadian Horseshoe Fall, Goat Island is situated, this divides the Mississippi[26] and thus forms the two Falls. Prospect House, where we stayed is just above the Horseshoe Fall. On arriving at the hotel the first thing was to have dinner, after this was over we repaired to the head of the falls and proceeded to go *under* it as far as possible. Before descending we had to put on a whole suit of oilskins. At length we got off. On arriving at the bottom with a guide we walked under the falls at least they call what is not under, by that name. I was very much disappointed with this part of the business, we were no more under the falls than fly. I was glad to get out of it. There was a good deal of snow frozen etc., and that was about all. The falls

26. This is geographically incorrect.

themselves are very grand as I said before, but this part of it was a *do*. We crossed over to the American side, the view from here too was very pretty. On retiring to bed, the latter was shaking like anything. They say the roar of the water can be heard 15 miles off, but I don't believe it. My bedroom looked on to the falls. Met Herbert, an old Rossallian here. Bye the bye in the afternoon, it was raining a little, the sun shining at the same time and a rainbow was shining right across the falls. It was very pretty. The Canadian Horseshoe falls are 1900 feet across and 150 feet high, being thus a great deal wider but not quite so high as the one on the opposite side. Three hundred million gallons of water are said to fall over in the hour.

May 4th.
Walked to see the rapids and whirlpool below the station in the morning. Was very much pleased. Could see the immense blocks of snow and ice being thrown over the Falls. After lunch we left the hotel to catch the 1.40 p.m. train for New York. Saw Hone, Webbe and Anderson there, they had just arrived from Chicago. Soon after leaving the station we passed Erie Lake on the right. It was covered with blocks of frozen snow being gradually carried down to the Falls and from thence into Lake Ontario. Passed through some very nice country.

May 5th.
Arrived at New York about 7.30 p.m. Drove to the Windsor Hotel. After breakfast Hornby, Penn and I went to see Mr. Soutter who had a good deal to do with St. George's Cricket Club. He took us to see the stock exchange. It was a wonderful sight, such a row I never heard, it was a mystery how they could transact business. Went round to see the different buildings, etc. Saw the Reredos in Trinity Church. It is very fine. Went to see "H.M.S. Pinafore" in the evening.

May 6th.
Went to the ground after lunch, had to cross the ferry to Hoboken where the ground is. Cholmondley Jones an old Magd. Coll. Oxon. called on me. Met young Kessler also of Manchester. Webbe etc. arrived from Niagara.

May 7th.

Began our match at Hoboken.[27] They gave us 4 men to make up the team. They only got 84. We made 234 for 5 wickets. Lucas 98, Penn 51, Self 31, Hornby 27 and Webbe 20. Met Phipps an old Ch. Ch.[28] man. Asked to go to a dance at the Franklyns 372 5th Avenue, but did not go.

May 8th.

Match continued, all out for 254. They only made 55 in their second innings. We thus won easily. Went to Niblo's Theatre in the evening. Very good ballet.

May 9th.

Major Deane, Webbe and I went over the river (Hudson) to Brooklyn to see the cemetery there. It is well worth seeing, being an immense place, very well kept. The view of New York from there is very good. Got back to the hotel about 2.30. Had lunch and went to see Webbe play Mr. La Montagne at Racquets. Webbe won easily. In the evening the New York Club gave us a dinner. It went off very well.

May 10th.

Left the Windsor Hotel about 7 a.m. in time to catch the White Star S.S. "Baltic" en route for Home. A beautiful morning. Left the wharf about 9. The "Brittanic" was just steaming up the harbour, having made a very good passage from Liverpool. Were delighted to find the sea perfectly calm on getting out into the open. Passed a very pleasant day, though rather slow. Got a beautiful cabin. Penn, Lucas, Webbe and I being together. Met an old Rossallian named Cradock on board. He was before my time, but introduced himself.

May 11th[29]

Sea still calm as a mill pond. Very cold. Passed heaps of vessels. The food on board is very good but the waiting tonight at dinner was wretched. The Captain read the service this morning in the saloon.

27. This match is not in *Wisden* but is reported in five columns in *The American Cricketer* for May 15, 1879. The English XI made 253.
28. Christ Church, Oxford.
29. By this time, the first-class season in England had already begun. Three of the tourists, Webbe, Ulyett and Emmett, would meet in the match between Middlesex and Yorkshire at Lord's on June 5.

Match Reports and Scores
Reprinted from
John Wisden's Cricketers' Almanack
for 1880

LORD HARRIS'S ENGLISH TEAM IN AUSTRALIA.

The visit of Lord Harris's team to Australia in our memorably severe winter of 1878-79, originated in an invitation from The Melbourne Club to The Gentlemen of England. That invitation was addressed to Mr. I. D. Walker, who, however, was then in India, consequently the correspondence on his behalf was undertaken by that gentleman's brothers, Mr. V. E. Walker and Mr. R. D. Walker. The visit was arranged, with the proviso of taking out two professionals if it was found impossible to get together a fairly representative team wholly composed of gentlemen. That proviso it was found necessary to act upon. Morley was asked, but declined to go; and the two professionals selected were George Ulyett and Thomas Emmett. The long illness, and subsequent death, of the brother of Mr. I. D. Walker prevented that gentleman becoming one of the team. Lord Harris kindly undertook the management, and after encountering various difficulties and disappointments, the following gentlemen and players agreed to make the visit and form

Lord Harris's Team.

Lord Harris (*Captain*).	Mr. F. A. Mackinnon.	Mr. A. J. Webbe.
Mr. C. Absolom.	Mr. H. C. Maul.	T. Emmett.
Mr. L. Hone.	Mr. F. Penn.	George Ulyett.
Mr. A. N. Hornby.	Mr. V. Royle.	
Mr. A. P. Lucas.	Mr. S. S. Schultz.	

The main body of this little cricketing army of England's—strong in batsmen and fieldsmen, but weak in slow bowling and wicket-keeping—left Southampton in the P. and O. ss. Australia on the 17th of October, 1878. On the midnight of Monday, December the 2nd, they arrived at the Semaphore in the R.M. ss. Assam, and were met at the Bay by the Adelaide reception Committee, and three gentlemen from Melbourne—representatives of the Melbourne Cricket Club—whose guests the Englishmen were. A four-in-hand drag took them to Adelaide that night, and on the following morning the Mayor of Adelaide gave them a most hearty welcome. A private Assembly Ball in honour of the Englishmen was held in the Town Hall on the 11th of December, at which Lady Jervois, His Excellency the Governor Sir William Jervois, and about 300 other ladies and gentlemen were present. The team had almost daily practice on the Association Ground up to the 12th, on which day they got into full cricketing harness, and commenced their first match :—

THE ENGLISH TWELVE v. EIGHTEEN OF SOUTH AUSTRALIA.

Played at Adelaide, December 12, 13, 14, 1878.—The weather was very hot, especially on the 14th. The attendances included Lady and Sir William Jervois on two of the days, and most of the notabilities, the public assembling in numbers, of more than 3,000 on the first day, 2,000 on the second day, and 4,000 on the third day—a day of intense heat unpleasantly accompanied by blinding clouds of dust. The match appears to have been most pleasantly played out in that manly, true spirit of cricket evinced by all thorough cricketers so conducive to the success of the game. The choice of innings was won by the South Australians, who commenced the batting. Their highest scorers were A. H. Jarvis, who made 28 and 8; T. Noel 1 and 33; W. Bullough 8 and 26; J. E. Gooden (*the Captain of the 18*) 14 and 8; J. Traynor 2 and 15; W. O. Whitridge 12 and 4; and J. Thurgurland 13 and 1. Noel's 33 included three 4's and two 3's; Jarvis's 28 included two 4's; Bullough's 26 was made by three 4's, one 3, two 2's, &c.; Traynor's 15 by two 4's, two 2's, &c.; and Thurgurland's 13 by two 4's, a three, and two singles. So the South Australians can hit a bit. They have also a most excellent wicket keeper in A. H. Jarvis; and they can bowl a bit. They made two fairly large innings, their totals being :—

THE SOUTH AUSTRALIAN EIGHTEEN...... 110, and...... 137.

Emmett's bowling had 14 wickets, three of which he *bowled down*, and 3 c and b Ulyett's bowling had 12 wickets, 8 of which he *bowled down*. Mr. A. J. Webbe caught out 5, and Mr. Hone stumped one and caught out another. The English batting was commenced by Mr. Lucas and Ulyett. The Yorkshireman was not fortunate; Mr. Hornby with 78 and 22 was highest scorer in both innings of England; his 78 was made by one 5, three 4's, three 3's, eight 2's, and so many (*for him*) as 36 singles; and his 22 included one 4, three 3's, and one 2. Mr. Webbe's 35 was made by a 5, five 4's, one 3, one 2, and 5 singles. Mr. Royle's 20 *not out* was made by 7 singles, five 2's, and a 3. Emmett's 16 included a 4 and three 2's, and his 6 not out was half-a-dozen singles. The local paper stated :—"*The two things for which the match will be memorable, are the wonderful fielding of Royle at cover point, and the batting of Hornby.*" The Englishmen won the match by 3 wickets. The following are the scores made by

THE ENGLISH TWELVE.

A. P. Lucas, l b w, b Bevan	12	— c Phillips, b Bevan	0
George Ulyett, c Thurgurland, b Bevan	0	— c Traynor, b Bevan	0
A. J. Webbe, c King, b Hide	35	— run out	6
Lord Harris, b Hide	9	— st Jarvis, b W. O. Whitridge	2
A. N. Hornby, c Jarvis, b W. O. Whitridge	78	— b W. O. Whitridge	22
F. A. Mackinnon, c Jarvis, b Hide	5	— c Jarvis, b W. O. Whitridge	2
V. Royle, run out	2	— *not out*	20
T. Emmett, c Phillips, b King	16	— not out	6
C. A. Absolom, c Pettinger, b W. O. Whitridge	12		
L. Hone, c Gooden, b Bullough	3		
H. C. Maul, not out	7	— run out	4
S. S. Schultz, b W. O. Whitridge	1		
Extras	5	Extras	1
	185		63

ENGLISH BOWLING.

	Overs.	Mdns.	Runs.	Wkts.		Overs.	Mdns.	Runs.	Wkts.
Emmett	44-1	18	45	9		56	38	58	5
Ulyett	23	15	17	3		48-3	33	43	9
Absolom	12	3	26	2		8	2	15	1
Lucas	4	—	8	—					
					Schultz	3	1	5	—

On the conclusion of the match Mr. Bundey, the Attorney-General, proposed the health of the visiting team, coupled with the name of Lord Harris. His lordship, in reply, thanked the people of Adelaide for their hospitality, and the Cricketing Association for their courtesy. The kindness displayed had made a marked impression on the mind of every member of the team, and he congratulated them on having played out a pleasant match in the true spirit of cricket. He was much surprised at the batting of some of the Eighteen, and he had no doubt but that in a few years they would turn out as good batsmen as there were in any other of the Colonies. Their bowling, he considered, would be a credit to many of the Counties, and when practising in the evenings he had seen more good fielders on the ground than would be seen at similar practices in England. His lordship concluded by proposing "Success to the South Australian Cricketing Association," coupled with the name of Mr. Gooden, and so, with a round of hearty cheers, terminated the visit of Lord Harris's team to Adelaide.

AT MELBOURNE.

The delegates of the Melbourne Cricket Club who met and welcomed the English Gentlemen at Adelaide, then accompanied them to Melbourne, where they arrived on Monday, the 16th of December, their reception being fully and graphically chronicled in *The Australian*, from which journal the following extracts are taken:—

"The Victorian on reaching Hobson's Bay was boarded by the President of the M.C.C., the Hon. T. G. Francis, and a numerous reception committee. Having landed, the party were driven to Melbourne in a four-in-hand drag. A considerable crowd had collected in front of the Melbourne Town Hall, and who greeted the visitors with hearty cheers, and when conducted to the Mayor's room, they were warmly welcomed to Melbourne by the Mayor, Mr. Councillor Story."

"Lord Harris, on behalf of the team, suitably "expressed their appreciation of the kind welcome accorded them, and to the M.C.C. for having sent delegates to receive them on their arrival at Adelaide." At the Victoria Club another welcome to Victoria was given to the team, the President of the Club, Sir T. O. Shaunessy, presiding. The Hon. J. Francis proposed "The Visitors," and in so doing remarked "Australians gloried in, rather than were ashamed of, the fact that one of the greatest defeats of the Australians in England was inflicted by the Gentlemen of England." (*Cheers*).

Lord Harris in responding expressed the thanks of the team for the warm welcome they had received; and, said his Lordship, "As to the contests between the Gentlemen of England and the Australian Eleven, he could not forget that though the Australians were defeated at Prince's, there was another match, in which, although it was drawn, the Australians had by no means the worst of it." (*Cheers and laughter*). Other courtesies passed until the time arrived for commencing the Englishmen's second match in Australia, *i.e.*,

THE ENGLISH ELEVEN v. FIFTEEN OF VICTORIA.

Played on the Melbourne Club Ground, December 26, 27, 28.—The Boxing day audience assembled to witness Lord Harris's team play their first match in Victoria numbered 10,000 at least. The weather was fine, and the wickets in magnificent run getting order, as may be imagined from the fact that when, after three days cricket, the match was drawn, there had been only three innings played for the 858 runs scored. The Victorians won choice, and began the batting. Four wickets had fallen for 51 runs, when Mr. Donald Campbell (of the Oxford University Elevens of 1874, '75, and '76) commenced his finely hit three figure innings of 128 runs—an innings that one journalist stated was "played without a chance," and another that it "comprised hits for thirteen 4's and eleven 3's." Mr. Campbell was eleventh man out, the score at 279; he was enthusiastically cheered by all on the ground. That day's cricket ended with the Victorians having lost 12 wickets and scored 288 runs.

Next day the innings ended early for 313 runs. At 12.45 Mr. Lucas and Ulyett commenced the English innings, and so successfully commenced it that when the first wicket (Ulyett's) fell the score stood at 85. Mr. Webbe was out at 133; and when 146 runs had been made a capital catch at point by the Victorian Captain, Mr. Allee, settled Mr. Lucas for 90—an innings that was chronicled as "first class cricket, without anything like a chance," and that included among other fine hits "a grand hit to leg, the ball bounding over the pavilion fence." Hearty cheers greeted Mr. Lucas's return from the wickets, and hearty cheering greeted Lord Harris's walk to them, but at 161 his Lordship was out. Mr. Hornby left at 189, and Mr. Mackinnon at 201. Mr. Royle hit freely for 78, and Emmett so carefully that his 26 included thirteen singles; and when time was up on that second day the English score stood at 304 for 8 wickets down. Mr. Absolom (3 not out), and Mr. Maul (2 not out).

The third day's play increased the English score to 331—or 18 on. Then the Victorians played a second innings of 214, whereupon time was up, and the match declared drawn, 38 wickets having fallen, 858 runs scored, 482 overs (less one ball) bowled, and the score left as follows:—

THE ENGLISH CRICKETERS IN AUSTRALIA.

The Fifteen of Victoria.

First Innings		Second Innings	
McDonnell, c Ulyett, b Emmett	21	b Ulyett	25
Gaggin, c Absolom, b Emmett	10	c Absolom, b Ulyett	11
Groube, st Hone, b A. P. Lucas	4	b Ulyett	13
Alexander, st Hone, b Emmett	6	c and b A. P. Lucas	43
Scott, b Ulyett	7	c Hone, b A. P. Lucas	22
Donald Campbell, run out	128	c A. J. Webbe, b Emmett	23
Elliott, c Royle, b Emmett	29	b Ulyett	3
Allee, st Hone, b Emmett	8	c Hornby, b Emmett	6
Tennent, c Absolom, b Emmett	5	b Ulyett	0
Terry, c Absolom, b Royle	5	run out	7
Slight, c and b Harris	19	b Ulyett	0
Trinnick, c Harris, b Emmett	13	c A. P. Lucas, b Emmett	8
Palmer, b A. P. Lucas	10	b Ulyett	5
McShane, not out	16	not out	14
Kendall, c Royle, b A. P. Lucas	4	c and b Ulyett	20
B 22, l b 3, w 3	28	B 8, l b 6	14
	313		214

The English Eleven.

A. P. Lucas, c Allee, b Scott	90
George Ulyett, run out	34
A. J. Webbe, c Palmer, b Scott	20
A. N. Hornby, c Elliott, b Palmer	21
Lord Harris, c and b McShane	8
V. Royle, c Palmer, b Allee	78
F. A. Mackinnon, b Palmer	4
Emmett, b Allee	26
C. A. Absolom, c Scott, b Palmer	21
H. C. Maul, b Palmer	5
L. Hone, not out	5
B 14, l b 5	19
	331

English Bowling.

	Overs.	Mdns.	Runs.	Wds.	Wkts.	Overs.	Mdns.	Runs.	Wkts.
Emmett	74	36	114	1	7	64	41	69	3
Ulyett	44	21	68	—	1	59	33	78	8
A. P. Lucas	33	13	59	—	3	15	4	37	2
Lord Harris	13	9	9	1	1	5	1	7	—
V. Royle	10	2	19	1	1	3	—	9	—
Absolom	4	—	16	—	—				

Victorian Bowling.

	Overs.	Mdns.	Runs.	Wds.	Wkts.
Palmer	40-3	13	72	—	4
McShane	30	9	65	—	1
Scott	29	9	55	—	2
Kendall	25	5	59	—	—
Alexander	15	5	24	—	—
Allee	10	—	22	—	2
Terry	8	4	15	—	—

AGAINST "THE AUSTRALIAN ELEVEN."

A week subsequent to the above match, Lord Harris's team commenced their third contest, and met their first defeat, their opponents on this occasion being the famous Australian Eleven who were so successful in England the preceding year. The Colonial team was the same that played in the old country, with the exception that Kelly played *v.* Bailey, who had previously met with an accident. The match was entitled :—

LORD HARRIS'S ELEVEN v. THE AUSTRALIAN ELEVEN.

Played on the East Melbourne Ground, January 2, 3, 4.—The ground was largely attended, 7,000 being present ere the day was out. His Excellency the Governor, and Lady Bowen, and Lady Harris, were among the company who filled every place of vantage for witnessing the match, deemed by all one of the most important in the programme. Lord Harris won choice, and, after due thought, chose his side should first bat, but his decision had hardly been given when rain fell freely for a short period. Mr. Lucas and Ulyett commenced the English batting; and so unfortunately was it commenced and continued, that the second ball delivered Ulyett played on before a run was scored. With the score at 6 Mr. Webbe was bowled; at 10 Mr. Lucas was bowled; and at 14 Mr. Hornby was bowled. Lord Harris stayed well, but when Mr. Royle had made three single's, Spofforth's bowling captured three wickets with three successive balls—the victims being Mr. Royle, Mr. Mackinnon, and Emmett, seven wickets being then down for 26 runs. Mr. Absolom was next man in; he forthwith played his old, old game of knocking the ball all over the ground, and with Lord Harris, increased the score to 89, when Garrett bowled his lordship for 33—a good innings; but Mr. Absolom continued hitting hard for the honour of the old land, until a capital catch at long field by A. Bannerman closed his score for 52, and England's innings for 113, Spofforth's bowling having taken 6 wickets *(4 bowled)* for 48 runs. Mr. Absolom's 52 was the biggest thing done with the bat for England in the match; his hits included five 4's, and both he, and his chief, Lord Harris, were as warmly, as they were deservedly, applauded.

Charles Bannerman and Murdoch began the Australian batting to the bowling of Ulyett and Emmett. Murdoch was soon settled. Charles Bannerman was out for 15, at 30; and when 37 had been scored Horan was had at wicket. Then A. Bannerman and Spofforth got together; Bannerman was missed by Mr. Hone at wicket before he had made a run, and Ulyett missed both batsmen, so they stayed together until "time" was called, the score then standing at 93, Spofforth *not out 35*; A. Bannerman *not out 23*. (One of the team wrote home:—"In fact I have seen more mistakes in these two matches at Melbourne than I expected to have seen all the time we were out. I can only account for it in the strong light here, the sky being so deep a blue that it dazzles our eyes, and you cannot judge a catch at all.")

Next day at noon the match was resumed, and when Spofforth had increased his score by four he was had by cover point. Garrett made 26, and was out at 131. And at 158 one of Mr. Hornby's grubs bowled Allan. Boyle stayed and helped A. Bannerman to make up the 200, the hoisting of which numbers elicited loud cheers, but shortly after Mr. Royle caught out Mr. Boyle for 28, mainly made by five 4's. Blackham and Kelly made brief stays, and when there was but one wicket to fall A. Bannerman played the ball on, and so was out for 73, the largest score hit in the match, and (after the chances) a fine innings that included eight 2's, four 3's, and seven 4's. Emmett bowled 59 overs for 68 runs, 7 wides, and 7 wickets.

The Englishmen's second innings was commenced by Mr. Lucas and Ulyett, to the bowling of Spofforth and Allan. They had made 26 runs, when Mr. Lucas was out from a capital catch by Boyle. Ulyett, Mr. Webbe, and Mr. Hornby were then quickly done with, four wickets being down for 34 runs; but Lord Harris and Mr. Royle stayed a bit; Mr. Royle was the first to leave, and just prior to "time" Lord Harris was caught out for 36—another good hit of batting, and the top score of that innings.

On the third day the English innings was resumed by Mr. Mackinnon and Mr. Absolom; neither stayed, but Emmett and Mr. Schultz did, the latter making 20, Emmett taking his bat out for 24; and so the score was hit to 160, and the one innings defeat averted by those two batsmen. The runs required by the Australians to win were then made by Charles Bannerman and Murdoch, and England was defeated by 10 wickets. Score:—

THE ENGLISH ELEVEN.

A. P. Lucas, b Allan	6	— c Boyle, b Allan	13
George Ulyett, b Spofforth	0	— b Spofforth	14
A. J. Webbe, b Allan	4	— l b w, b Allan	0
A. N. Hornby, b Spofforth	2	— b Spofforth	4
Lord Harris, b Garrett	33	— c Horan, b Spofforth	36
V. Royle, b Spofforth	3	— c Spofforth, b Boyle	18
F. A. Mackinnon, b Spofforth	0	— b Spofforth	5
T. Emmett, c Horan, b Spofforth	0	— *not out*	24
C. A. Absolom, c A. Bannerman, b Boyle	52	— c and b Spofforth	6
L. Hone, c Blackham, b Spofforth	7	— b Spofforth	6
S. S. Schultz, not out	0	— c and b Spofforth	20
B 4, l b 2	6	B 10, l b 4	14
	113		160

THE ENGLISH CRICKETERS IN AUSTRALIA.

THE AUSTRALIAN ELEVEN.

Charles Bannerman, b Emmett	15
W. L. Murdoch, c A. J. Webbe, b Ulyett	4
T. Horan, c Hone, b Emmett	10
A. Bannerman, b Schultz	73
F. R. Spofforth, c Royle, b Emmett	39
T. Garrett, c Hone, b Emmett	26
F. Allan, b Hornby	5
H. Boyle, c Royle, b Emmett	28
J. Blackham, b Emmett	6
T. J. D. Kelly, c A. J. Webbe, b Emmett	10
D. Gregory, not out	12
B 19, l b 2, w 7	28
	256

THE AUSTRALIAN'S 2ND INNINGS:—Charles Bannerman, not out, 15. Murdoch, not out, 4. Total 19.

AUSTRALIAN BOWLING.

	Overs.	Mdns.	Runs.	Wds.	Wkts.		Overs.	Mdns.	Runs.	Wkts.
Spofforth	25	9	48	—	6	....	35	16	62	7
Allan	17	4	30	—	2	....	28	11	50	2
Boyle	7	1	11	—	1	....	10	4	16	1
Garrett	5	—	18	—	1	....	10	6	18	—

ENGLISH BOWLING.

	Overs.	Mdns.	Runs.	Wds.	Wkts.		Overs.	Mdns.	Runs.	Wkts.
Ulyett	62	24	93	—	1					
Emmett	59	31	68	7	7	....	1	—	9	—
A. P. Lucas	18	6	31	—	—					
A. N. Hornby	7	7	—	—	1					
S. S. Schultz	6-3	3	16	—	1	....	2	—	10	—
V. Royle	4	1	6	—	—					
Lord Harris	3	—	14	—	—					

IN TASMANIA.

The Englishmen's fourth match was played in Tasmania—a spot of this round cricket ball shaped earth that Tom Emmett praised all round, saying "The Tasmania climate is one of the finest I ever enjoyed, you don't experience the hot winds nor the dust or sand storms as you do in Victoria or New South Wales, nor do they suffer from the quantity of rain they have in New Zealand. Fruit grows in abundance, and as we were leaving Hobart Town a gentleman got into the train with a basket of cherries such as I never before saw for size, and of a flavour as good as any I have tasted." (What a paradise). This fourth match of the series was entitled—

THE ENGLISH ELEVEN v. EIGHTEEN OF SOUTHERN TASMANIA.

Played on the Association Ground, at Hobart Town, January 9, 10, 11.—IN THIS MATCH Emmett's bowling captured 15 (*10 bowled*) of the 34 Tasmanian wickets, and Ulyett's 11 wickets (*10 bowled*) for 44 runs. Only one Tasmanian, Davies, made double figures in their first innings, but in their second they played some good cricket, their largest scorers in the match being T. G. Davies, with 13 and 23; W. H. Walker, with 8 and 33; E. T. Freeman, with 7 and 29; and J. Aitken, with 3 and 17 not out. The results of their batting were—

EIGHTEEN OF SOUTH TASMANIA, 82 *and* 144.

The English Eleven for this match included Mr. F. Penn, who, however, was not fortunate in this his first match in the Colonies; but others were. Mr. Lucas made 26 and 45 *not out;* Ulyett 13 and 22; and Mr. Hornby 61 *not out;* and the Englishmen won by 6 wickets, the following being the score of

THE ENGLISH CRICKETERS IN AUSTRALIA.

THE ENGLISH ELEVEN.

A. P. Lucas, b H. V. Bayley	26	—	not out	45
George Ulyett, c Wright, b E. H. Butler	13	—	c E. H. Butler, b Martin	22
A. J. Webbe, c Freeman, b Boddam	3	—	b H. V. Bayley	4
A. N. Hornby, *not out*	61	—	c H. V. Bayley, b Boddam	3
Lord Harris, b H. V. Bayley	0	—	not out	13
F. Penn, b H. V. Bayley	1	—	b H. V. Bayley	4
T. Emmett, run out	1			
V. Royle, b Boddam	5			
C. A. Absolom, run out	4			
L. Hone, b Boddam	5			
H. C. Maul, c and b Boddam	0			
Extras	14		Extras	3
	133			94

ENGLISH BOWLING.

	Overs.	Mdns.	Runs.	Wkts.		Overs.	Mdns.	Runs.	Wkts.
Emmett	25	9	33	9		43	23	51	6
Ulyett	18	8	24	2		32	23	20	9
Lucas	8	4	18	4		16	6	26	1
Absolom	2	1	1	—		5	1	15	—
					Royle	3	—	6	—

TASMANIAN BOWLING.

	Overs.	Mdns.	Runs.	Wkts.		Overs.	Mdns.	Runs.	Wkts.
E. F. Boddam	34-3	8	65	4		10	2	32	1
H. V. Bayley	27	13	34	3		22-1	9	30	2
E. H. Butler	8	1	20	1		7	—	14	—
					W. Martin	5	1	15	1

The next match was a one day affair. It was entitled—

THE ENGLISH ELEVEN v. EIGHTEEN OF NORTH TASMANIA.

Played at Launceston, January 13.—EMMETT WAS FRIGHTFULLY SEVERE with his bowling in the Eighteen's first innings, taking 12 of their wickets—7 bowled—for 20 runs, Major Cox, with 18, being the only double figure scorer for Tasmania in the match, their totals being

EIGHTEEN OF NORTH TASMANIA, 49 *and* (7 wickets down) 38.

In the Englishmen's innings Mr. F. Penn (in form) was top scorer with 53; Lord Harris made 33; Mr. C. A. Absolom 32; Emmett 24; and Ulyett 22; the total being 212, *vide* the following score of

THE ENGLISH ELEVEN.

A. P. Lucas, b Atkinson	0
George Ulyett, b T. Hogg	22
A. N. Hornby, c Hales, b Atkinson	8
Lord Harris, c Ferguson, b Longman	33
F. Penn, c Douglas, b Ferguson	53
V. Royle, b Ferguson	5
T. Emmett, c Watson, b W. Hogg	24
C. A. Absolom, b Ferguson	32
H. C. Maul, b Ferguson	0
L. Hone, b Douglas	12
S. S. Schultz, not out	15
B 5, w 3	8
	212

ENGLISH BOWLING.

	Overs.	Mdns.	Runs.	Wkts.
Emmett	34	16	20	12
Ulyett	30	14	22	5
Lucas	4-3	2	3	—

The English bowling in this partly played-out innings did come to hand.

Six Tasmanians bowled. The most successful were Ferguson, who obtained 4 wickets for 32 runs; and Atkinson, who had 2 wickets for 34 runs.

THE ENGLISH CRICKETERS IN AUSTRALIA.

IN NEW SOUTH WALES.

ON THE 17TH OF JANUARY the Englishmen started for Sydney, where they anticipated meeting as strong a team as they had done at East Melbourne; for their fresh foes for this match included Evans, whose reputation as a bowler is second to none in the Colonies; and Massie and R. C. Allen, rising batsmen; the former being thought by many good judges to be equal in batting to Charles Bannerman, which is "thinking" a great deal. This, the sixth match, was played level handed, and was entitled—

THE ENGLISH ELEVEN v. THE NEW SOUTH WALES ELEVEN.

Played at Sydney, January 24, 25, 27, 28.—The wickets must have been in good form for batting, and, perhaps, the bowling was also; for there were so many as 27 double figure scores made; seven scores of 50, or more, runs hit; and (despite some fine fielding) 931 runs made for the 35 wickets down in the match. Those 931 runs being made from 589 overs. Spofforth met with an accident to one of his wrists and could not play; and Charles Bannerman played with two of his fingers bound up owing to an accident when fielding previously. Gregory, for some reason or other, was left out of the Sydney Eleven, their Captain being Murdoch, who played in big form, scoring more runs than any other man in this great run-getting match. The Englishmen began the batting, and through the fine hitting of Ulyett, Lord Harris, and Mr. F. Penn—all of whom made 50—they scored an innings of 248 runs. The N. S. W. men then made 16 without losing a wicket, when the first day's play ceased. Next day Emmett's bowling quickly settled the two not outs of the preceding evening, and Ulyett bowled Charles Bannerman for 0; but Murdoch made 70, Evans 21, Thompson 50, and Massie 30; those four men being mainly instrumental in working the total up to 240, or only eight short of the Englishmen's first innings. In their second innings nine of the Englishmen scored double figures, but none got above 29, and the total closed at 217, or 225 on. In the Sydney men's second innings four men went out for few runs; but Murdoch again scored well, this time making 49; and when Massie faced Charles Bannerman their good batting fairly, and finely, won the match for their side, *Charles Bannerman taking his bat out for 60,* and *Massie taking his out for 78.* Bannerman's hits included five 4's (three in succession), and a hit into the Pavilion inclosure for 5; and such enthusiasm did his hitting evoke that—said *The Sportsman*—"*A collection resulting in the nice little sum of £140 was made, and presented to Charles Bannerman.*" And so it came about that the New South Wales Eleven won this match by 5 wickets. Score:—

THE ENGLISH ELEVEN.

George Ulyett, c Thompson, b Tindall	51	— st Murdoch, b Evans	20
A. P. Lucas, c and b Tindall	7	— b Coates	15
A. J. Webbe, c Allen, b Coates	1	— l b w, b Coates	27
A. N. Hornby, c A. Bannerman, b Evans	12	— b Evans	20
Lord Harris, b Evans	50	— c A. Bannerman, b Tindall	22
F. Penn, c Garrett, b Coates	56	— c Garrett, b Evans	18
V. Royle, c A. Bannerman, b Tindall	12	— b Coates	29
T. Emmett, c Garrett, b Tindall	9	— not out	16
C. A. Absolom, c Seale, b Tindall	17	— c Allen, b Evans	22
L. Hone, c Garrett, b Tindall	16	— c Thompson, b Evans	0
S. S. Schultz, not out	13	— b Coates	1
Extras	4	Extras	27
	248		217

THE NEW SOUTH WALES ELEVEN.

A. Bannerman, c Lucas, b Emmett	28	— b Lucas	15
T. Garrett, c Absolom, b Emmett	12		
Charles Bannerman, b Ulyett	0	— not out	60
W. Murdoch, c A. J. Webbe, b Ulyett	70	— b Lucas	49
E. Evans, l b w, b Lucas	21	— c Emmett, b Lucas	1
D. Thompson, b Emmett	50	— c Hornby, b Ulyett	9
R. C. Allen, b Lucas	0	— c Hone, b Ulyett	5
H. H. Massie, run out	30	— not out	78
J. Seale, st Hone, b Emmett	0		
J. Coates, st Hone, b Lucas	2		
Tindall, not out	9		
Extras	18	Extras	9
	240		226

THE NEW SOUTH WALES BOWLING.

	Overs.	Mdns.	Runs.	Wkts.	Overs.	Mdns.	Runs.	Wde.	Wkts.
Tindall	60-3	26	89	6	31	13	44		1
Evans	41	16	68	2	67-1	34	82		5
Coates	22	5	52	2	25	14	38		4
Garrett	12	2	35	—	20	6	26		—

THE ENGLISH BOWLING.

	Overs.	Mdns.	Runs.	Wkts.	Overs.	Mdns.	Runs.	Wde.	Wkts.
Emmett	64	32	70	4	43	22	51	1	—
Lucas	35-1	16	53	3	54	24	76	—	3
Ulyett	31	16	51	2	33	18	57	—	2
Schultz	21	8	43	—	9	2	18	—	—
Hornby	4	3	2	—	13	8	15	—	—
F. Penn	3	1	3	—					

From Sydney the team proceeded to Bathurst, where they commenced their seventh match, *i.e.* :—

THE ENGLISH ELEVEN v. EIGHTEEN OF BATHURST.

Played at Bathurst, January 31, February 1.—THE EIGHTEEN began the batting, but the bowling of Mr. Lucas and Emmett got them out for an innings of 47 runs (including 4 extras), the highest scorer among them being A. Docker with 11 not out. Mr. Lucas's bowling had 8 wickets—*4 bowled*; and Emmett's 7 wickets—*6 bowled.* Mr. A. J. Webbe kept wicket and stumped two men out for 0 each. When one innings each side had been played the match was left unfinished, the following being the score made by—

THE ENGLISH ELEVEN.

H. C. Maul, b West	18	Lord Harris, b A. Docker	0
F. A. Mackinnon, st Bonar, b Cassidy	15	A. J. Webbe, c Clarke, b West	26
George Ulyett, c Ferguson, b West	32	A. N. Hornby, not out	24
F. Penn, c Turner, b A. Docker	32	T. Emmett, b A. Docker	8
V. Royle, run out	4	C. A. Absolom, b A. Docker	19
A. P. Lucas, c T. Docker, b A. Docker	21	Extras	30
			229

AT SYDNEY AGAIN.

THE ENGLISHMEN THEN LEFT BATHURST FOR SYDNEY, and when there enjoyed some excellent batting practice for their eighth match, the return between

THE ENGLISH ELEVEN v. THE NEW SOUTH WALES ELEVEN.

Played on the Association Ground, at Sydney, February 7, 8, 10, 1879.—The weather was splendid. On the first day it was recorded there were 4000 persons present, including Lady Robinson and party. On the second day, a Saturday, and the day of disturbance, it was reported there were fully 10,000 persons present; but on the third day (Monday) there were not more than 1,500 on the ground.

The Englishmen having won choice, commenced the batting on good wickets, with Hornby and Lucas, to the bowling of Spofforth and Evans. They made a truly great stand, for, notwithstanding several bowling changes, the score was hit to 125 before the first wicket fell by Spofforth bowling Lucas for 51—chronicled in in *The Australasian* as "A fine exhibition of cricket, he did not give a chance all through." When but 7 more runs had been added, Spofforth also bowled Hornby for 61—stated to have been "A fine innings, with only one possible chance." Ulyett and Lord Harris then made another good stand, as they increased the score from 132 to 217 ere they were separated by Ulyett being magnificently caught out for 55 by Evans close to the pavilion fence. Touching this catch, *The Australian* remarked, "Ulyett hit a ball from Spofforth towards the pavilion enclosure; Evans running at full speed made a kangaroo-like bound at the flying leather, and secured it with one hand. The performance of course brought down the house." With the score at 234 Evans bowled Lord Harris for "a fine innings of 41 runs." Then came a collapse, for the fifth wicket also fell at 234, the sixth at 235, the seventh at 247, the eighth at 255, the ninth at 262, and the tenth at 267. Soon after the third wicket fell Charles Bannerman had to retire from fielding, consequent on the reopening of a wound on his hand received in a previous match. It may here be stated that Hornby's 67 included seven 4's; Lucas's 51, four 4's; Ulyett's 55, seven 4's; Lord Harris's 41, four 4's; and Penn's 13, two 4's. The N.S.W. innings was commenced by A. Bannerman and Murdoch to the bowling of Lucas and Schultz, who were subsequently relieved by Emmett and Ulyett, and in the latter's first over A. Bannerman was out for 16 (including three 4's), the score standing at 34 for that first wicket. At 37 Thompson was out, whereupon Massie faced Murdoch, and when (in a bad light) the stumps were drawn for that day the Sydney score stood at 53 for two wickets, Murdoch, *not out*, 28.

On the Saturday the not outs resumed their innings about noon, to the bowling of Lucas and Emmett, the former being subsequently succeeded by Ulyett, and he by Hornby, who, later on, clean bowled Massie for 38—an innings that included four 4's. The score was at 130 when Massie was bowled. Then Emmett's bowling had a good time, inasmuch as it captured the remaining seven wickets, the innings closing for 177 runs, *Murdoch having triumphantly played all through the innings, taking his bat out for 82*—described "a grand innings." Murdoch's hits were eleven 4's, three 3's, nine 2's, and 11 singles. Emmett's bowling in that innings summed up 52 overs (less one ball) for 47 runs and 8 wickets. Being in a minority of 90 runs, the N.S.W men, in due course, "followed on," Murdoch and A. Bannerman commencing their second innings. 19 runs had been made, 10 of them by Murdoch, when an appeal to Coulthard, the Umpire, resulted in Murdoch being run out, then arose

THE DISTURBANCE

that *The Australasian* remarked would "for ever make the match memorable in the annals of New South Wales cricket." It appears that on the decision being given Murdoch (like a true cricketer) retired; whereupon arose cries of "Not Out!"—"Go back, Murdoch!"—"Another Umpire!" and so on. The crowds rushed to the wickets, and, stated *The Australasian*, "rowdyism became rampant for the rest of the afternoon." The Eleven Englishmen were surrounded by a rough and excited mob, who prevented further cricket being played that day. Much was said and written on this deplorably disgraceful affair; but it is gratifying to record that all respectable portions of Australian society, and all the leading journals in the Colonies strongly condemned this outrage. *The South Australian Register* stated "The scene was a disgrace to the people," *and* "profound regret is expressed at the occurrence." *The Sydney Mail* remarked, "The English team soon found themselves in the centre of a surging, gesticulating, and shouting mob, and one rowdy struck Lord Harris across the body with a whip or stick." *The Australasian* stated "His Excellency, Lady Robinson, and party were present, and were pained witnesses of all that occurred;" *and* "The disgraceful affair was the talk of the town;" furthermore, *The Australasian* headed a report with "What will they say in England?" *The South Australian Chronicle* chronicled the remark that "Such a scene had never before been witnessed on a cricket field." And in a subsequent edition, *The Australasian* added—"Before the game was resumed on the Monday, Mr. R. Driver (President of the Cricket Association), Mr. F. H. Dangar, and others, waited upon Lord Harris, and on behalf of the cricketers of Sydney expressed their extreme regret at the disgraceful scene that took place on the Saturday. The Captain of the English team, in reply, said, 'he did not place any blame on the Association, or the cricketers of Sydney, but it was an occurrence which it was impossible he could forget.'"

The Sydney Morning Herald of February 27, said:—"Our English readers will be glad to learn that steps have been taken to wipe out the disgrace of the discreditable attack on Lord Harris and his cricketers. William Rigney and John Richards were recently charged at the Water Police Court with having participated in the disorder arising in consequence of Murdoch being declared out by the Umpire for the English team. Both men expressed deep regret for what had occurred, and pleaded guilty, and it was in consideration of this rather tardy contrition, and the good character given them by the police that the Bench fined them 40s., and to pay 21s. professional costs, and 5s. costs of Court. Mr. Driver, who appeared for the prosecution, stated that inmates of the pavilion who had initiated the disturbance, including a well-known book-maker of Victoria who was at the time ejected, had had their fees of membership returned to them, and they would never again be admitted to the ground. The Bench referring to the kindly hospitable treatment the Australian cricketers received in England, expressed deep regret that Lord Harris and his team should have met such a disagreeable experience."

On Monday, the third day, play was resumed at 12.20. In the interim the wickets had been softened by heavy rainfalls; none made a stand but A. Bannerman who (*first man in*) was ninth out, the score at 49, his 20 being made by three 4's, one 2, and six singles. The tenth wicket fell with the score unaltered, so the Englishmen won by an innings and 41 runs, Emmett's bowling having taken 5 wickets for 21 runs, and Ulyett's 3 for 13 runs. Score:—

THE ENGLISH ELEVEN.

A. N. Hornby, b Spofforth	67	V. Royle, c and b Evans	6
A. P. Lucas, b Spofforth	51	C. A. Absolom, c and b Evans	6
George Ulyett, c Evans, b Spofforth	55	S. S. Schultz, c and b Evans	5
Lord Harris, b Evans	41	L. Hone, not out	4
F. Penn, c Massie, b Spofforth	13	Extras	19
A. J. Webbe, b Evans	0		—
T. Emmett, c Evans, b Spofforth	0		267

THE NEW SOUTH WALES ELEVEN.

W. Murdoch, *not out*	82	— run out	10
A. Bannerman, c Royle, b Ulyett	16	— c A. J. Webbe, b Emmett	20
N. Thompson, c Lucas, b Emmett	3	— c F. Penn, b Emmett	0
H. H. Massie, b Hornby	38	— b Emmett	8
Charles Bannerman, c F. Penn, b Emmett	9	— c Hornby, b Emmett	4
E. Evans, b Emmett	5	— c Emmett, b Ulyett	1
D. Gregory, c Ulyett, b Emmett	4	— c A. J. Webbe, b Ulyett	0
E. Sheridan, c Schultz, b Emmett	0	— b Emmett	0
F. Spofforth, b Emmett	0	— c A. J. Webbe, b Ulyett	0
E. Powell, c Hone, b Emmett	5	— not out	0
E. Tindall, l b w, b Emmett	0	— c F. Penn, b Emmett	0
Extras	15	Extras	6
	—		—
	177		49

Umpires—Mr. E. Barton for N. S. W., and Coulthard for England.

THE NEW SOUTH WALES BOWLING.

	Overs.	Mdns.	Runs.	Wkts.	Overs.	Mdns.	Runs.	Wkts.
Spofforth	44	12	93	5				
Evans	38	13	62	5				
Tindall	27	6	79	—				
Thompson	11	4	14	—				

THE ENGLISH BOWLING.

	Overs.	Mdns.	Runs.	Wkts.	Overs.	Mdns.	Runs.	Wkts.
Emmett	51-3	27	47	8	28	13	21	6
Hornby	22	13	24	1	5	2	9	—
Ulyett	17	4	44	1	22	15	13	3
Lucas	12	4	20	—				
Schultz	15	5	27	—				

Any notice of this match would be inexcusably incomplete that left out two important documents subsequently published, *i.e.*,—Lord Harris's letter to a friend that appeared in the London newspapers early in April, and The New South Wales Cricket Association's reply to that letter, published in the London newspapers the last week of July. Space in this little book can ill be spared for these letters, but they are deemed of such import that the compiler has no choice but to chronicle them. Here follows a copy of

LORD HARRIS'S LETTER.

"I am not certain whether you will be astonished or not at what I have to tell you, but I know you will be distressed that your friends, a party of gentlemen travelling through these Colonies for the purpose of playing a few friendly games of cricket, should have been insulted and subjected to indignities it distresses us to look back upon. We began the return match with the N.S.W. Eleven on Friday, February 7, scored 267, and got our opponents out for 177 by 3.30 on the Saturday afternoon. Murdoch, who had carried his bat out in the first, and A. Bannerman went to the wickets to commence the second innings. At 19 on the telegraph the former was run out. Before he got back to the pavilion I heard shouts of "not out," "go back," &c., arise from that quarter, and saw the occupants of it rise almost *en masse.* I at once saw what was the matter, and instead of waiting for D. Gregory (the captain) to come out to me, perhaps unwisely walked to the pavilion to meet him at the gate. He, I found, in the name of the N.S.W. E'even, objected to Coulthard, the umpire. I must here diverge to explain certain facts connected with umpires in t ese Colonies which are not known or understood at home. Contrary to *our* custom, it is here the exception to employ professional umpires. This I was not told until *after* the disturbance. As you know, we brought no umpire, and on arrival at Adelaide I asked the representatives of the Melbourne C.C. if they could recommend anyone to us whom we could take about with us throughout our tour. They mentioned this man Coulthard, a professional on their ground, whom they had constantly tried and found competent, and added that if we *on trial* also considered him competent, the M.C.C. would be very glad to give him leave of absence so long as we wanted his services. I considered him on trial a good and trustworthy umpire, and arranged with the M.C.C. that he should accompany us to N.S.W. Had we known on our arrival that a feeling existed in these Colonies against the employment of professional umpires, it is possible we might have acted differently; but, understand, at the same time, that I have seen no reason as yet to change my opinion of Coulthard's qualities, or to regret his engagement, in which opinion I am joined by the whole team. To resume my account of the disturbance on the ground on the Saturday. I asked Gregory on what grounds the objection was raised, and he said at first general incompetence, but afterwards admitted that the objection was raised on account of the decision in Murdoch's case. I implored Gregory, as a friend, and for the sake of the N.S.W. Cricket Association, which I warned him would be the sufferer by it, not to raise the objection, but he refused to take my view of the case. Looking back in the midst of this conversation, I found the ground had been rushed by the mob, and our team was being surrounded. I at once returned to the wickets, and in defending Coulthard from being attacked was struck by some 'larrikin' with a stick. Hornby immediately seized this fellow, and in taking him to the pavilion was struck in the face by a would-be deliverer of the 'larrikin,' and had his

C

shirt nearly torn off his back. He, however, conveyed his prisoner to the pavilion in triumph. For some thirty minutes or so I was surrounded by a howling mob, resisting the entreaties of partisans and friends to return to the pavilion until the field was cleared, on the grounds that if our side left the field the other eleven could claim the match. I don't suppose that they would have done so, but I determined to obey the laws of cricket, and may add that for one hour and a half I never left the ground, surrounded during the whole time, with two short intervals, by some hundreds of people. At about five o'clock the crowd was cleared off somehow. I then took the opinion of the Eleven as to changing the umpire, and it was decided *nem. con.* that there were no grounds for the objection, and that we should decline to change him. I informed Gregory of the decision, whereupon he said, 'Then the game is at end.' On Coulthard appearing from the pavilion groans arose from the crowd, and at the same moment it began to break the ring again. The two batsmen who had been standing at the wickets returned to the pavilion, re-called, I afterwards found, by Gregory, but at the time I thought possibly because of the threatened irruption of the crowd. I turned to Mr. Barton, the N.S.W. Eleven umpire, and asked if I could not claim the match according to the laws of cricket. His answer was, 'I shall give it you in two minutes' time if the batsmen do not return.' I said to him, 'I won't claim it yet. I'll give the other side every chance of reconsidering a decision arrived at, I believe, unadvisedly, and in a moment of passion. Please ask Gregory what he means to do." On returning Mr. Barton informed me that Gregory would send two men to the wickets—a curiously sudden change of mind I think you will allow. However, before the batsmen could appear the crowd had covered the ground for the second time. After some twenty minutes it was cleared for the second time also. A. Bannerman and Thompson then took their places at the wickets, but before a ball could be bowled the crowd broke in for the third and last time. I remained on the ground until the time for drawing the stumps, surrounded as before. Beyond slyly kicking me once or twice the mob behaved very well, their one cry being, 'Change your umpire.' And now for the cause of this disturbance, not unexpected, I may say, by us, for we have heard accounts of former matches played by English teams. It was started and fomented by professional betting men in the pavilion, members of the association. The disgraceful part of the business is that other members of the association—one a member of the legislative assembly—aided and abetted the bookmakers in raising the cry. I blame the N.S.W. eleven for not objecting to Coulthard before the match began, *if* they had reason to suppose him incompetent to fulfil his duties. I blame the members of the association (many, of course, must be excepted) for their discourtesy and uncricket like behaviour to their guests; and I blame the committee and officers of the association for ever permitting betting, but this last does not, of course, apply to our match only. I am bound to say they did all in their power to quell the disturbance. I don't think any thing would have happened if A. Bannerman had been run out instead of Murdoch, but the latter, besides being a great favourite, deservedly I think, was the popular idol of the moment through having carried his bat out in the first innings. As a contrast to the reception the Australian Eleven met with after beating the M.C.C. at Lord's, I may say that when we won the match on Monday, hardly a cheer was given us by the ring. The occupants of the pavilion acknowledged our victory. They are capital winners out here, but I am afraid I can't apply the same adjective to them as losers. To conclude, I cannot describe to you the horror we felt that such an insult should have been passed on us, and that the game we love so well, and wish to see honoured, supported, and played in an honest and manly way everywhere, should receive such desecration. I can use no milder word. The game was finished on Monday without interruption. Coulthard had made two mistakes in our first innings, one favouring us, the other the opposite. Murdoch's decision was considered by cover-point and point to be a good one, and I repeat that the N.S.W. Eleven had no grounds whatever for raising an objection. We never expect to see such a scene of disorder again—we can never forget this one.

"I remain,

"Yours sincerely,

"February 11." "HARRIS.

THE ENGLISH CRICKETERS IN AUSTRALIA.

THE NEW SOUTH WALES CRICKET ASSOCIATION'S REPLY.

(Contributed to *The Daily Telegraph* by Mr. J. M. Gibson, the hon. secretary to the Association).

"A few days ago a letter from Lord Harris, published in your issue of April 1, appeared in the Colonial Press. That letter dilated upon a lamentable disturbance which occurred at Moore Park, near this city, during a match played between his lordship's eleven and an eleven of New South Wales, on February 7, 8, and 10 last. Upon the appearance of the letter in our newspapers a feeling of indignation was generally expressed, and within a few hours a requisition influentially signed was presented, calling on me to convene a special general meeting of the New South Wales Cricket Association for the purpose of considering the letter and comments made upon it in some of the London papers. A meeting was accordingly convened, and took place this evening. The President, Mr. Richard Driver, M.P., occupied the chair, in the presence of an unusually large attendance of members. The letter referred to having been read, and the President, Sir George Innes, M.L.C., Mr. M. H. Stephen, Q.C., Mr. G. H. Reid, and Mr. Richard Teece having addressed the meeting, it was unanimously resolved that I should ask you to publish the following statement, in correction of the account transmitted by Lord Harris, which, principally upon the following grounds, is universally regarded here as both inaccurate and ungenerous.

"When Lord Harris prepared his letter of February 11, he was fully aware of the following facts:

"1. That on the previous day a deputation from the association, consisting of our president, some of the vice-presidents, officers, and members waited upon him, and expressed profound sorrow and regret for the conduct of the unruly portion of the crowd, and Lord Harris was pleased to assure the deputation that he did not hold the association in any way responsible for what had occurred.

"2. That immediately after the disorder on the cricket ground the public and the press were loud in their indignation at the occurrence, and assured our visitors of their utmost sympathy; and the team received similar marks of good feeling from all quarters.

"3. That betting on cricket matches is strictly prohibited by the trustees of the ground, so far as it can be so prohibited, and large placards to that effect have always been kept posted throughout the pavilion and its inclosures.

"Lord Harris, by what we feel to be a most ungenerous suppression of these facts and others, has led the British public to suppose that in New South Wales, to quote his own words, 'a party of gentlemen travelling through these colonies for the purpose of playing a few friendly games of cricket should have been insulted and subjected to indignities,' whilst the press and inhabitants of Sydney neither showed surprise, indignation, nor regret. We cannot allow a libel upon the people of New South Wales so utterly unfounded as this to pass without challenge. The country upon which such a reproach could be fastened would be unworthy of a place among civilised communities, and in the imputation is especially odious to Australians, who claim to have maintained the manly, generous, and hospitable characteristics of the British race.

"Having shown that for what actually occurred the fullest acknowledgments were made, it is now right to point out that the misconduct of those who took possession of the wickets has been exaggerated. So popular amongst our people is the game of cricket that multitudes of all ages and classes flock to a great match. They watch these contests with an interest as intense as any felt in England over a great political question. Lord Harris is, we believe, the first English cricketer who failed to observe that they applaud good cricket on either side, and, so far from our crowds being the bad losers he represents, the English Elevens who have visited New South Wales were never made more of than when they defeated the local team. Previous decisions of the professional brought from Melbourne to act as umpire for the English Eleven had created real, though suppressed dissatisfaction, and one, giving Lord Harris a second 'life,' was openly admitted by his lordship to be a mistake; and when Mr. Murdoch, the hero of the hour, who had carried his bat

C 2

through in the first innings, was at the crisis of the game given 'run out' by what a large proportion of the spectators, both in the pavilion and round the inclosure, as well as the batsman himself, whether rightly or wrongly, took to be a most unfair decision, the excitement and indignation of a section of the spectators, led by the juvenile element, unhappily broke through restraint. Only once before in New South Wales was a cricket ground rushed, and then, as in the present instance, the crowd was seized with a conviction of foul play. But the present demonstration was entirely against the umpire, whom Lord Harris still considers competent, whilst admitting 'he had made two mistakes in our innings.' It certainly was not against our gallant visitors. The only cry was 'Change your umpire!' and the mob voluntarily left the ground more than once in the hope that that would be done. The betting men to whom Lord Harris alludes, and of whom only one or two were present, were not members of this association at all, and it is completely unjust to assign the demonstration to any such agency. Bad as it was, it sprang from no mercenary motive.

"Sydney, June 4th."

A week subsequent to the Sydney match, the English gentlemen enjoyed two days' hard hitting when playing:

ELEVEN ENGLISH GENTLEMEN v. FIFTEEN OF THE BOHEMIAN CLUB

at Yarra Bend on the 17th and 18th of February. THIS MAY BE RECKONED BY SOME PEOPLE as an affair outside the English programme; nevertheless the compiler thinks fit to chronicle it as the Englishmen's ninth match. F. Penn unfortunately dislocated his knee, and was thereby deprived of the pleasure of playing again for Lord Harris's team in Australia, an accident, and a loss, much regretted by all who knew this fine batsman, and esteemed gentleman. However, the English gentlemen made a lot of runs, and for the matter of that so did "The Bohemians," for in the three innings (two not fully played out) 745 runs were scored. G. P. Robertson (of the Oxford University Eleven of 1866) led the lot with 78 and 28 for "The Bohemians." A. J. Webbe was a good second with 62 for England; and among a cluster of good scores well up at the finish were:—S. S. Schultz with 55; A. Campbell with 46 *not out*; R. Chirnside with 45; A. P. Lucas with 41; Lord Harris with 40; and D. Campbell with 32. The journalists were good enough to publish a bowling analysis of the three innings; but as in one innings' summary the runs were 15 too few, and in all three summaries the maiden overs were out of all possible proportion to the overs bowled, such analysis is declined with thanks, so all that can be added is the following score:—

THE FIFTEEN OF THE BOHEMIAN CLUB.

A. F. Robinson, c Harris, b Lucas	23	— b Absolom	17
D. Campbell, c Harris, b Lucas	0	— b Hornby	32
W. H. Moule, c Absolom, b Schultz	3	— run out	7
G. Wilkie, run out	9	— b Schultz	19
W. McEvoy, c A. J. Webbe, b Lucas	11	— run out	0
W. Ford, c Absolom, b Lucas	1	— c Lucas, b Hornby	4
E. Fanning, c Mackinnon, b Hornby	16	— b Absolom	0
A. Loughnan, c Royle, b Hornby	19	— c Hornby, b Absolom	12
G. P. Robertson, c Schultz, b Royle	78	— c sub., b Hornby	28
R. Chirnside, c Absolom, b Lucas	0	— st A. J. Webbe, b Royle	45
H. Jennings, st A. J. Webbe, b Lucas	0	— c Schultz, b Harris	15
A. Campbell, c and b Schultz	6	— *not out*	46
D. Wallace, c Lucas, b Hornby	19	— c A. J. Webbe, b Schultz	3
T. Quirk, b Harris	11	— not out	8
W. F. Darke, *not out*	22		
Extras	10	Extras	26
	228		262

THE ENGLISH CRICKETERS IN AUSTRALIA.

THE ENGLISH ELEVEN.

A. J. Webbe, c A. Robinson, b Ford	62
F. A. Mackinnon, c Wallace, b Moule	4
S. S. Schultz, b D. Campbell	53
A. P. Lucas, c Jennings, b D. Campbell	41
A. N. Hornby, c Quirk, b McEvoy	0
Lord Harris, c A. Campbell, b D. Campbell	40
V. Royle, *not out*	21
G. H. Maul, st Wilkie, b D. Campbell	8
C. A. Absolom, b D. Campbell	1
L. Hone, b Moule	11
F. Penn (*met with accident, and could not play*)	
Extras	14
	255

The Englishmen then proceeded to Melbourne, there to play level handed—man for man—against the Victorians, a match that occupied four days in playing, and "all but" run into one of a thousand runs. This their tenth match was

THE ENGLISH ELEVEN v ELEVEN OF VICTORIA.

Played at Melbourne, February 21, 22, 24, 25.—THE ENGLISHMEN lost the valuable aid of F. Penn, and the Victorians had no professionals in their team. The weather on the first day (Friday) was dull, cold, breezy, and cheerless, and this combined with its being "mail day" at Melbourne, limited the attendance to about 1,800. England began the batting with Lucas and Hornby, to the bowling of Allan and Boyle. The batsmen made so good a stand for the old country, that when the first wicket fell, by Hornby being bowled off his pads for 50, the score was at 89. Hornby's 50 was stated to have been "scored in his best style;" it included four 4's, and 18 singles. Lucas and Lord Harris then hit the score to 115, when Lucas was bowled by Cooper for 38, twenty of which runs were made by fourers. Ulyett was next man in, but at 131 Lord Harris was stumped for 26; and at 134 A. J. Webbe was bowled for 3. Thereupon Emmett faced Ulyett, and the two Yorkshiremen became so troublesome to the Victorians, that despite various bowling changes, they enlarged the score by 86 runs, for when Ulyett was bowled the figures were 220 for 5 wickets. Ulyett's 71 included eight 4's and six 3's, his innings being chronicled as "a very fine free hitting display." Emmett and Royle played the score from 220 to 268; then the Yorkshireman was settled by the man at mid-on for 41, described "a good and steady innings," made by five 4's (three in succession), three 3's, &c. Royle and Absolom made yet another stay for the honour of the old land, as when Absolom was stumped for 20, the score was at 305 for 7 wickets. The light was then bad for batting. Mackinnon was stumped at 310, and shortly after Royle was also stumped, his 57 being praised as "a very good innings, his leg-hitting being especially noticeable." Royle's 57 included eight 4's and three 3's. Hone, last man in, was also stumped by *Blackham, who, in that innings, stumped out 5 of the 10 Englishmen.*" The English innings ended for 325 runs, the largest number scored by them in this series of matches. In the half-hour's cricket played in the queer light of that evening the Victorians lost one wicket (Allan's) and scored two runs.

On the Saturday the weather was unfavourable, but about 4,000 visitors were present. Cooper and Groube resumed the innings. With the score at 3 only Groube was had at slip, and at 9 Cooper was bowled. Horan and Baker then increased the runs to 42, when Horan was out for 26, four 4's (three in succession) looming largely in his score. At 80 Baker was out for 31, mainly made by two 4's, three 3's. and 10 singles. Campbell and Alexander stayed so profitably for their side that they increased the score from 80 to 136, when a slow ball from Emmett clean bowled Alexander for 24. Campbell hit freely, but at 154 Boyle was out for 3; and as 7 wickets were then down the hope of saving the "follow on" was not an encouraging one to the Victorians, but hope on, hope while there is a man left to fight, is a good battle cry at cricket. Blackham then faced Campbell, and the score was hit to 170 when Campbell was out (from a fine catch of Ulyett's at the chains) for 51, a steadily played and most useful innings that included four 4's and ten 2's. Major was next man in; he played well until the figures were 209, when he was l b w for 24, and thereby let in the last of the Victorians—Moule,—and, amid much excitement, Moule and Blackham stayed until 261 were scored, when Blackham was run out for 46, so many as seven 4's being included in that innings. The weather and light were bad when the Englishmen commenced their second innings, having then just one hour of time to play out. When only 13 runs had been made Lucas was out; at 19 Hornby was out; and at 44 Lord Harris was out. Ulyett and Webbe then made the score 59, when play ceased for that day.

The Monday was a beautiful day, and the ground was attended by about 4,000 visitors. Ulyett and Webbe went on with the England innings, but with the score at 82 Webbe was out for 20. Ulyett and Emmett played it up to 116, when Alexander bowled Ulyett for another "fine free hitting innings," this 48 being made by seven 4's (three of them successive hits), &c. Ulyett's three last hits were a 3, a 4, and a 3. At 118 Emmett was run out for 20, made by two 4's and six 2's. Royle made 13 by three 3's and a 4. But nine men were out when only 139 runs were scored. Then Mackinnon and Hone carefully increased the runs to 171, when Boyle bowled Hone for 22, and so England's second innings was ended. The Victorians then required 236 runs to win. When 25 runs had been made Emmett bowled Alexander for 17; at 34 Emmett bowled Groube for 12; and at 42 Moule was c and b by Lucas for 6. Campbell then faced Horan, who gave a chance to slip from Emmett's bowling, but the chance was not taken, and, said *The Australasian*, "The miss was a dear one," as indeed it was, for the two batsmen hit freely, profited by more escapes, and moved the score to 133, when Emmett bowled Campbell for 37, made by a leg hit for 5 from Absolom, four 4's, three 2's, &c. At 137 Baker was out; and at 147 Blackham was out. Horan and Boyle then increased the score to 178, when Horan was l b w for what *The Australasian* termed "a lucky, but very useful innings of 69 runs." His hits included two 5's, and five 4's. Major then went to wickets, but the stumps were shortly after drawn, the score at 178 for 7 wickets.

The Tuesday was a fine and a warm day, but there were not more than 1,000 people present. Play was not commenced until 2 o'clock, and when it did commence the English fielding was not of good form, so the result was defeat. Boyle and Major increased the score to 208, when Boyle was bowled for 26, a fortunate innings that included so many as nine 2's. Eight wickets were then down and 28 runs wanted to win when Allan faced Major, who shortly after was missed being stumped, and returned thanks therefore by cutting one from Emmett for 3, and driving one from Absolom over the chains for 5, and so they went on scoring until a hit to leg for 3 by Major won the match for the Victorians by two wickets; Allan not out 14, and Major *not out* 27, made by a 5, a 4, three 3's, three 2's, and three singles.

In this match 15 different bowlers (9 Victorians, and 6 English) bowled an aggregate of 569-3 overs (2,279 balls) for 912 runs from the bat. The extras numbered 81. Emmett bowled 138 overs. Score:—

THE ENGLISH ELEVEN.

A. P. Lucas, b W. H. Cooper	38	— c Baker, b Allan	1
A. N. Hornby, b Alexander	50	— c Allan, b W. H. Cooper	8
Lord Harris, st Blackham, b W. H. Cooper	26	— c Blackham, b W. H. Cooper	8
George Ulyett, b Horan	71	— b Alexander	48
A. J. Webbe, b Allan	3	— c Campbell, b Boyle	20
T. Emmett, c Boyle, b Moule	41	— run out	20
V. Royle, st Blackham, b W. H. Cooper	57	— b Alexander	13
C. A. Absolom, st Blackham, b W. H. Cooper	20	— b Alexander	2
S. S. Schultz, st Blackham, b W. H. Cooper	2	— b Allan	5
F. A. Mackinnon, not out	5	— not out	10
L. Hone, st Blackham, b Boyle	2	— b Boyle	22
B 5, l b 4, n b 1	10	B 8, l b 6	14
	325		171

ELEVEN OF VICTORIA.

F. Allan, b Emmett	0	— not out	14
W. H. Cooper, b A. P. Lucas	0		
J. Groube, c Absolom, b Emmett	2	— b Emmett	12
T. Horan, c Absolom, b A. P. Lucas	26	— l b w, b Absolom	69
F. Baker, c Royle, b Ulyett	31	— c Royle, b Absolom	2
D. Campbell, c Ulyett, b A. P. Lucas	51	— b Emmett	37
G. Alexander, b Emmett	24	— b Emmett	17
H. Boyle, c Royle, b Emmett	3	— b Emmett	26
J. Blackham, run out	46	— c Hone, b A. P. Lucas	6
G. Major, l b w, b Emmett	24	— *not out*	27
W. Moule, not out	17	— c and b A. P. Lucas	6
B 27, l b 8, w 1, n b 1	37	B 10, l b 7, w 3	20
	261		236

VICTORIAN BOWLING.

	Overs.	Mdns.	Runs.	Wds.	N. b.	Wkts.	Overs.	Mdns.	Runs.	Wds.	Wkts.
Allan	34	13	63	—	—	1	37	17	57	—	2
Cooper	29	3	79	—	—	5	27	8	46	—	2
Alexander	29	8	50	—	—	1	17	8	22	—	3
Boyle	22-3	8	48	—	—	1	13	8	20	—	2
Moule	8	—	24	—	—	1					
Campbell	7	5	8	—	—	—					
Major	7	1	18	—	1	—	5	1	12	—	—
Horan	5	1	15	—	—	1					
Baker	3	2	10	—	—	—					

ENGLISH BOWLING.

	Overs.	Mdns.	Runs.	Wds.	N. b.	Wkts.	Overs.	Mdns.	Runs.	Wds.	Wkts.
Emmett	63	34	93	1	—	5	75	46	53	3	4
Lucas	43	21	43	—	—	3	43	20	72	—	2
Ulyett	26	7	56	—	1	1	11	4	18	—	—
Absolom	18	9	21	—	—	—	21	10	37	—	2
Hornby	6	3	5	—	—	—	7	1	15	—	—
Schultz	5	3	6	—	—	—	8	3	21	—	—

The Englishmen's next and eleventh match was against a Twenty-two team, a match that was remarkable for the stubborn defence shown by a young batsman among the Twenty-two; for the large number of runs scored before the first English wicket fell, and for Hornby hitting the only three figure score made in this series of matches. The match was

THE ENGLISH ELEVEN v. TWENTY-TWO OF BENDIGO AND DISTRICT.

Played on the Back Creek Cricket Ground, at Sandhurst, February 26, 27.—A HOT WIND BLEW CLOUDS OF DUST across the ground on the first day, but on the second day a change in the wind made the weather pleasant. The Bendigo men began the batting. In their first innings Hartley made 25, Findlay 21, Harry 15, and "*a young player named Bruce showed very dogged defence, being at the wickets over one hour and a half for 7 runs.*" (If 7 runs in 90 minutes be this youngster's true form, what a nice mate he would make for Barlow; Bruce and Barlow, first men in, with Tupp to follow first wicket down, would start an innings in a form that would drive some bowlers half crazy). In the Bendigo men's second innings Beswick made 31, G. Mackay 27, Spargo 15, and Bruce 6. (The chronicler did not state how long Bruce was at wickets in making those half-dozen runs). This second innings was not quite played out, there being one wicket to fall when time was up. The totals were:—

BENDIGO'S 1ST INNINGS...... 141. 2ND INNINGS (*20 wickets down*)...... 161

The English batting was commenced by Hornby and Mackinnon in remarkable form, inasmuch as when time was up on the first day, the English score stood thiswise:—

A. N. HORNBY,	*not out*	77
F. A. MACKINNON,	*not out*	45
Extras		16
No wicket down		138

Next day Mackinnon added one run to his 45 and was then out, but Hornby made his score 104, the only three figure score made in these matches. Others scored moderately well, but the above was the cream of the hitting shown in the following innings played by

THE ENGLISH ELEVEN.

A. N. Hornby, st Smith, b Manalick	104
F. A. Mackinnon, c Smith, b Manalick	46
A. J. Webbe, run out	11
L. Hone, c Smith, b G. Mackay	23
H. C. Maul, run out	22
A. P. Lucas, c Findlay, b Butler	14
George Ulyett, c Butler, b Manalick	13
V. Royle, c Hartley, b Manalick	6
Lord Harris, c and b Neill	20
T. Emmett, b Butler	26
C. A. Absolom, not out	1
B 16, l b 2	18
	304

THE ENGLISH BOWLING.

	Overs.	Mdns.	Runs.	Wds.	Wkts.	Overs.	Mdns.	Runs.	Wde.	Wkts.
Emmett	44-1	16	45	4	7	48-3	13	59	1	8
Ulyett	39	15	34	—	7	41	13	43	—	6
Absolom	11	—	23	—	4	24	6	36	—	3
Lucas	9	1	18	—	—	6	2	4	—	—

The twelfth match played by the team was

THE ENGLISH ELEVEN v. TWENTY-ONE OF BALLARAT.

Played on the Ballarat Oval on the Saturday and Monday, March 1 and 3.—THE WEATHER WAS FAVOURABLE, and the attendances good. Lord Harris won choice of innings, and the Englishmen began the batting; they hit well and scored largely in the first half of their innings, but later on the slow bowling of W. H. Figgis obtained three wickets for few runs, the last six wickets making but 44 of the 296 from the bat. The following is the innings scored by

THE ENGLISH ELEVEN.

A. N. Hornby, b Brokenshire	86
A. P. Lucas, c E. Figgis, b Cleverley	24
Lord Harris, c Franklin, b Brokenshire	89
A. J. Webbe, run out	53
George Ulyett, c Antcliffe, b Duffy	12
V. Royle, b W. H. Figgis	5
H. C. Maul, hit wicket	5
T. Emmett, c Scales, b W. H. Figgis	9
L. Hone, run out	5
C. A. Absolom, not out	5
S. S. Schultz, c Keogh, b W. H. Figgis	3
Extras	15
	311

The Ballarat batsmen scored fairly well; E. Figgis made 9 and 9; C. Sherard, 14 and 14; C. Nettle, 24 and 19; and Lewis, 21 and 28; and touching the last mentioned two innings, *The Australasian* said, "For Ballarat a lad named Lewis—quite a boy—played splendidly in both innings, scoring 21 in his first innings and 28 in his second, playing the bowling with the utmost confidence. He was heartily cheered by the Englishmen on his retirement in each innings." Lewis was caught out both innings. The totals were :—

BALLARAT, 1ST INNINGS, 140. 2ND INNINGS (one man absent), 123.

So the English Eleven won by an innings and 48 runs.

THE ENGLISH BOWLING.

	Overs.	Mdns.	Runs.	No b.	Wkts.	Overs.	Mdns.	Runs.	Wkts.
Emmett	59	24	54	1	11	39	12	58	9
Schultz	39	15	30	—	5	29	14	21	4
Ulyett	11	—	32	—	—	20	11	14	5
Lucas	10	2	10	—	1	10	—	21	—
Absolom	1	—	5	—	—				

The Englishmen's thirteenth and last match in Australia was a level handed and successful fight against the Victorians, that Eleven including the famous Aboriginal cricketer JOHN MULLAGH, whose very fine batting in England in 1868 (especially his splendid 75 at Lord's on the 12th of June of that season) earned him so large a portion of popularity among the cricketers of the old Country. The match was

THE ENGLISH ELEVEN v. ELEVEN OF VICTORIA.

Played at Melbourne, March 7, 8, and 10.—ON THE FIRST DAY (Friday) the weather was fair, the wickets in good order, the fielding ground fast, and the attendance up to 5000, including His Excellency the Governor, and a large assemblage of ladies. The Englishmen commenced the batting so disastrously that when only 3 runs had been made Cooper caught out Hornby; and when but 8 had been scored Mullagh caught out Lucas. But then so fine a front was shown by Lord Harris and A. J. Webbe, that they worked the score to 100, when away went three good wickets clean off the reel, Webbe being had at slip by the new bowler, Palmer, who immediately backed up that success by clean bowling Lord Harris and Emmett; the third, fourth, and fifth wickets thus all falling with the score at 100. Webbe's 24 was finished off with three successive 4's, and Lord Harris's 67 (a very finely hit innings) included a great drive over the chains for 5, and nine 4's—three in succession. Ulyett and Royle then stayed and hit so well that they moved Old England's score from the 100 to 199, when Palmer bowled Ulyett for 47—a fine innings, that included four 4's and but 5 singles. Royle (in at the 100) stayed until 236 had been made; then Palmer bowled him for 75—"a splendid hitting display," *that—by a 4, a 4, a 4, and a 2—included 14 runs from one over of Boyle's*, and altogether included eleven 4's. At 240 "a terrific break-back" from Palmer bowled Absolom; and at 242 another break-back from Palmer bowled Hone. Then Boyle bowled Schultz, and so was the innings finished for 248, Palmer's bowling having captured 6 English wickets (*all bowled*) for 64 runs. Slight and Alexander began the Victorian batting to the bowling of Ulyett and Emmett. The wicket-keeper caught out Alexander before a run had been made; when 5 had been scored a rare fine bail ball from Emmett bowled Slight, and when 15 had been booked Campbell was out from a good catch at deep square leg made by Hone. Horan and Blackham were then together; and despite the bowling of Lucas, Emmett, Ulyett, Schultz, and Absolom, they increased the score to 84, when Schultz bowled Horan for 46—an innings that included four 4's and 18 singles. With the score at 101

Lord Harris caught out Blackham for 39, three 4's and the same number of 3's being the principal hits therein. Baker was out at 110, and the day's play ceased with the Victorian score at 112 for 6 wickets down.

The Saturday was bright, breezy, balmy, and altogether beautiful, and about 9,000 visitors were on the ground. Boyle and Moule resumed the innings and moved the score to 127, when Lucas bowled Moule. John Mullagh played carefully for 4 when Emmett bowled him; Boyle was out for 17, and the innings closed for 146, Emmett's bowling having captured 6 wickets (*3 bowled*) for 41 runs and 4 wides. The Victorians "followed on" with Slight and Baker, to the bowling of Emmett and Absolom. At 19 Slight was caught out by cover-point for 8; Baker and Boyle then hit the score to 42, when another catch by Royle settled Baker for 17. Campbell's play was steadiness itself whilst Horan hit the score to 63, when still another catch by cover-point ended Horan's innings for 31, the principal hits being three 4's and 9 singles. Blackham hit one from Absolom well away for 4, but was then l b w, the score at 67. Then Mullagh went to wickets, and played in his old, steady, careful, and excellent form, but he quickly lost the company of Campbell, who was out from yet one more catch by cover-point, Royle having caught out at cover-point four of the five wickets then down. (35 runs had been added to the score during Campbell's long stay at wickets for 2). Mullagh and Alexander then made a stand for Victoria; they brought on several bowling changes, and the score to 122, when Hornby bowled Alexander for 31, twenty of which runs were made by five 4's. At 126 Boyle was bowled by Hornby; at 131 Palmer was out; at 142 Moule was out; and as there was then only one wicket to fall, all hoped Mullagh would carry out his bat, but it was not to be, for shortly after Schultz bowled him for 36, and the innings was over for 155. Mullagh's 36 was a good display of patient, careful, and skilled batting. His hits included four 4's, and so pleased were the lookers-on with his batting that, said *The Australasian*, "*A subscription was started for him on the ground, and a sum of £50 soon collected*."

At 5.15 the Englishmen commenced their second innings requiring 54 runs to win. The light was bad for batting, especially so at one end, and the wickets went down so fast, that, when the score was at 10 Hornby played on; at 15 Palmer bowled Mackinnon *and* Ulyett, both with "Yorkers," and at 23 Palmer bowled Lord Harris. Webbe and Lucas increased the score to 30 "when play ceased for the night." ("Some slight misunderstanding arose as to the time for drawing the stumps, but the matter was amicably arranged after a short discussion.")

On the Monday play was resumed at 11.15, and in a short time Webbe and Lucas made the necessary winning runs, so the English Eleven won this last match in Australia by 6 wickets, "A result," said *The Australasian*, "well deserved by them, and worthily obtained by splendid play both with the bat and in the field. Webbe took his bat out for 22, made by two 4's, three 3's, one 2, and 3 singles, and Lucas's 21 *not out* was commenced with two successive 4's, and concluded with a 3. Score:—

THE ENGLISH ELEVEN.

A. P. Lucas, c Mullagh, b Alexander	6	— *not out*	21
A. N. Hornby, c W. H. Cooper, b Alexander	2	— b Alexander	2
Lord Harris, b Palmer	67	— b Palmer	6
A. J. Webbe, c Palmer, b Boyle	24	— *not out*	22
George Ulyett, b Palmer	47	— b Palmer	0
T. Emmett, b Palmer	0		
V. Royle, b Palmer	75		
F. A. Mackinnon, not out	15	— b Palmer	2
C. A. Absolom, b Palmer	4		
L. Hone, b Palmer	1		
S. S. Schultz, b Boyle	0		
B 3, l b 3, n b 1	7	L b 1	1
	248		54

THE ENGLISH CRICKETERS IN AUSTRALIA.

The Eleven of Victoria.

	1st		2nd	
J. Slight, b Emmett	1	—	c Royle, b Emmett	8
G. Alexander, c A. J. Webbe, b Emmett	0	—	b Hornby	31
T. Horan, b Schultz	46	—	c Royle, b Emmett	31
D. Campbell, c Hone, b Lucas	5	—	c Royle, b Emmett	2
J. Blackham, c Harris, b Emmett	39	—	l b w, b Absolom	4
F. Baker, c Royle, b Emmett	10	—	c Royle, b Emmett	17
H. Boyle, b Lucas	17	—	b Hornby	2
W. Moule, b Lucas	13	—	b Schultz	2
John Mullagh, b Emmett	4	—	b Schultz	36
G. Palmer, not out	0	—	c Harris, b Emmett	0
W. H. Cooper, b Emmett	0	—	not out	1
B 4, l b 3, w 4	11		B 10, l b 7, w 4	21
	146			155

The Victorian Bowling.

	Overs.	Mdns.	Runs.	Wds.	No b.	Wkts.		Overs	Mdns.	Runs.	Wds.	Wkts.
Boyle	45-2	7	44	—	—	2						
Palmer	34	13	64	—	1	6	......	20	8	30	—	3
Alexander	31	14	52	—	—	2	......	19	8	23	—	1
W. H. Cooper	19	4	48	—	—	—						
Horan	4	1	9	—	—	—						
Moule	4	2	16	—	—	—						
Mullagh	3	—	8	—	—	—						

The English Bowling.

	Overs.	Mdns.	Runs.	Wds.	No b.	Wkts.		Overs	Mdns.	Runs.	Wds.	Wkts.
Emmett	46-2	27	41	4	—	6	......	52	23	68	4	5
Lucas	25	11	32	—	—	3	......	9	3	20	—	—
Ulyett	22	13	20	—	—	—	......	5	3	6	—	—
Absolom	10	3	17	—	—	—	......	22	8	23	—	1
Schultz	9	1	25	—	—	1	......	5	2	8	—	2
Hornby							......	15	11	9	—	2

So ended the cricket played in the Australian Colonies by Lord Harris's team in 1878-'79. How they played, what matches they won, lost, or left unfinished, is amply detailed (for a book of this dimension and purpose) on preceding pages, rendering it unnecessary to occupy further space about the trip, beyond recording that on the evening of the 8th of March, the M.C.C. entertained Lord Harris and his team to a farewell dinner at the Victoria Club, His Excellency the Marquis of Normanby being also one of the guests. *The Australasian* recorded the dinner—"A great success every way. Lord Harris made a straightforward, manly speech, which commended itself to all his hearers, and the whole affair passed off with the greatest *éclat*."

In the following week the members of the team left Australia for Old England, some by one route, others by another, and in due time all arrived safe and hearty at that blessed haven so dear to all true Englishmen—HOME.

N.B.—The compiler of this book desires to thankfully acknowledge how materially he is indebted to *The Australasian* for the information recorded on the preceding pages, and he also tenders his earnest thanks to those few kind friends in the Colonies who so obligingly sent him other items.